Joseph M. Webb

Chalice Press
St. Louis, Missouri

All scripture quotations, unless otherwise indicated, are from the *New Revised Standard Version Bible,* copyright 1989, Division of Christian Education of the National Council of the Churches of Christ in the USA. Used by permission.

Scripture quotations marked (NIV) are taken from the *Holy Bible, International Version©.* NIV©. Copyright © 1973, 1978, 1984 by International Bible Society. Used by permission of Zondervan Publishing House. All rights reserved.

Cover design: Michael A. Domínguez
Art direction: Michael A. Domínguez
Interior design: Elizabeth Wright

This book is printed on acid-free, recycled paper.

Visit Chalice Press on the World Wide Web at
www.chalicepress.com

10 9 8 7 6 5 4 3 2 1   98 99 00 01 02 03

Library of Congress Cataloging-in -Publication Data

Webb, Joseph M., 1942–
    Comedy and preaching / by Joseph M. Webb.
        p.   cm.
    Includes bibliographical references.
    ISBN 0-8272-0475-2
    1. Preaching. 2. Comic, The—Religious aspects—Christianity. 3. Wit and humor—Religious aspects—Christianity.   I. Title.
    BV4235.H85W43 1999   98–44959
    251—dc21   CIP

Printed in the United States of America

For Jerry Adams,
my original comic brother.

A gentle man laughing.

Acknowledgments

More than anything else, this book is the product of twenty-some years of preaching—all but a few of those years week-end preaching, since I taught at various colleges, universities, and seminaries for most of that time. It was in those churches, though, that I learned both the value and the dynamics of the comic spirit in the pulpit. So as I turn loose of a book that I have wanted to write for a long time, my mind and my heart encircle those people who, over the years, have shared Sundays with me: to the young, vibrant families of the Agoura Hills Christian Church in suburban Southern California (where I met my friend and comrade Jerry Adams); to the little band of intrepid farmers and their families of the Dot Christian Church in the hills of Virginia; to the inner city and street folk of the West Main Street Christian Church in Johnson City, Tennessee; to the struggling but determined congregation of First Christian Church in Fontana, California; and to the wondrous fellowship of retired and elderly people who are the First Christian Church of Hemet, California, where I preached before joining the Claremont faculty. I am grateful, too, for Jon Berquist, my editor at Chalice Press; his great humor and warmth, to say nothing of his editorial skills, are unfailing. Finally, I must express gratitude for the abiding friendship of Fred Craddock, teacher and mentor to so many of us. This book is an effort to pay tribute in some small way to both his insights and his Christian character. He not only taught us; he has shown us how.

Contents

Preface

*What keeps our faith cheerful is the extreme persistence of
gentleness and humor. Gentleness is everywhere in daily life,
a sign that faith rules through ordinary things: through
cooking and small talk, through storytelling, making love,
fishing, tending animals and sweet corn and flowers, through
sports, music and books, raising kids—all the places where the
gravy soaks in and the grace shows through. Even in a time of
elephantine vanity and greed, one never has to look far to see
the campfires of gentle people. If we had no other purpose in
life, it would be good enough to simply take care of them and
goose them once in a while.*

Garrison Keillor[1]

There is no way to know if Mr. Keillor, the American humorist, had the work of the preacher—and preaching—in mind when
he wrote those words, but he certainly could have. What he did
not say either, but again could have, was that whenever one happens to catch a glimpse of some gentle people around a campfire,
one always hears the unmistakable sound of laughter. Laughter
and campfires go together. Laughter and gentle people go together.

To talk about laughter is to talk about humor; it is to talk about
comedy or the comedic. Like laughter, they are as difficult to define or pin down as the air itself. We can make distinctions, and in
this book we shall explore some that have been made, some that
have particular relevance for our work as ministers and preachers.
Humor and comedy, for example, are certainly correlated with
each other, though they are by no means synonymous. Conrad
Hyers, who is probably the preeminent Christian scholar in the
area of humor and comedy, writes that humor "represents those
attitudes and moods—identified by such words as caprice, frivolity, levity, jest, and facetiousness—that are expressed in the
various types of comic structure: farce, burlesque, buffoonery,

ix

joking, clowning, etc. In the comic spirit, humor is the spirit, comedy the form; and laughter is its overt expression."[2]

It would be easy to begin a book like this for the preacher by simply lifting a very funny paragraph from a good preacher's recent sermon and saying: "There! Look at that! See how much fun that was? You can actually hear the people laughing when that was said from the pulpit." Mind you, a lot of such paragraphs exist; not a few preachers reading this right now could pull out a number of funny paragraphs from their own sermons. What needs to be said, though—at least at this point—is that the idea of humor or comedy as part of the sermon is a very controversial notion, and one is tempted to say "still" a very controversial notion. It is a controversy that must be taken seriously since, even for those of us who value and embrace the comedic spirit in preaching, the elements of the controversy provide some necessary cautions about comedy to which every pulpit must pay heed.

Still, we need to start, in a sense, at the beginning, at least as far as the notion of comedy is concerned. There is a reason, theoretically at least, why Christianity and comedy might not have hit it off well right away. The word "comedy" is Greek, after the Greek god, Comus, who was honored regularly with an elaborate ritual procession. It was an unabashed fertility rite, since Comus was a fertility god. Comus was the symbol of perpetual rebirth, the symbol of life without end. A certain notoriety surrounded Comus and the fertility festival which was, in many ways, among the most exuberant celebrations of regeneration in all of Greek culture. Not surprisingly, when the Greek term *komus* appears in the New Testament, which it does at three places, it is always used in a highly negative sense of carousing and reveling, a meaning that had obviously become well established in the Greek lexicon. Twice Paul the apostle warns against walking in the revelings of *komus*—in Romans 13:13 and Galatians 5:21—while yet another such warning occurs in 1 Peter 4:3.

Whatever the nature or origins of the term itself, though, it clearly came to be used to express something profoundly elemental within the human species, something that Suzanne Langer, the brilliant philosopher of language and art, called the "human life-feeling," an immediate and intense "sense of life," an experience of sheer "exhilaration."[3] If one is able to grasp the idea of *komus* outside the bounds of the New Testament, outside the bounds of Paul's spirit-body dualism, one grasps an effort among the ancients to understand the mysterious interactions, the comic rhythms, of divine and human—a "life-feeling," as Langer puts it, that is "at once religious and ribald, knowing and defiant, social and freakishly individual."[4] Laughter, in a sense, came to symbolize that inseparable rhythm of spirit and body, since it was clear that laughter required both, that laughter sprang from something within and yet had no means of expression apart from the convulsive movements, whether large or small, of the body itself.

Moreover, the Greeks—who cannot be said to have "originated" such things, since laughter preceded the Greeks—devised highly structured forms for stage and arena designed to maintain and ensure as much as possible the perpetuation of these inexplicable life forces of soul and body that seemed always to be connected in some way to the process of laughter and merriment. Langer discusses this joyous "rhythm of animal existence" as the ancients' way of confronting "the strain of maintaining a vital balance amid the alien and impartial chances of the world, complicated and heightened by passionate desires." As a result, she says, comedy must be understood as

> an art form that arises naturally wherever people are gathered to celebrate life, in spring festivals, triumphs, birthdays, weddings, or initiations. For it expresses the elementary strains and resolutions of animate nature, the animal drives that persist even in human nature, the delight [humanity] takes in its special mental gifts that make [it] the lord of creation; it is the image of human vitality holding its own in the world amid the surprises of unplanned coincidence.[5]

Langer's work is concerned primarily with the creation of art forms, in this case the comedic form. Early on in our study, we shall be concerned with what others will call the comedic "vision" or "perspective," a way of looking at life itself. We shall call it the comic spirit. But Langer provides us with a powerful metaphor for tying together a general comedic viewpoint and the creation of comedic art. She writes: "Because comedy abstracts and reincarnates for our perspection, the motion and rhythm of living, it enhances our vital feeling, *much as the presentation of space in painting enhances our awareness of visual space.*"[6] The role of the visual arts in our lives is to give us new ways of "seeing" and appreciating the visual dimensions of life itself. One can, in this sense, talk about "art for art's sake," finding in it its own pleasures and enjoyments, its own aesthetic satisfactions; one can also talk about art as having a larger "function," whether intended by the artist or not, an "awareness-building" function. It is the *focusing* of experience, its concentration in a small, highly developed space, that "teaches us" to see, as it were, "on our own" in the activities of living. For Langer, comedic art does the same thing: Constructed, controlled comedy, the comedy of stage or screen, can be appreciated and enjoyed on its own, for its own sake as the joy of laughter; or, it can be understood as a way to grasp life through a comedic lens, to see the comedic wherever one looks. In truth, Langer would have art, even comedic art, not as one or the other, but as both. Through comedic art, one develops a comedic "vision"; one's comedic vision, in turn, provides one with an intense enjoyment of comedic art.

One of the problems in any analysis of humor or comedy is its virtually unlimited range of form and expression. There appears to be no end to the causes of laughter. We laugh whenever we find something, anything, "funny," at someone's joke or pratfall, at a party or celebration, at a funny movie or play, at the antics of another person, at our children trying on adult hats and clothes. We laugh at others; we laugh at ourselves; we laugh just because others are laughing, even though we are not sure why they are. We laugh when someone physically tickles us, though we usually prefer not to, since such laughter often carries with it a kind of physical pain. It is not that we do not know what causes us to laugh—we do.

Virtually anything can cause us to laugh, given the right circumstances. We are not talking about one thing, but about a thousand things. That is what makes the comedic so difficult to define. Comedy is everywhere. It exists in every culture, from the simple to the most complex. It exists as miming, as clowning, as joke-telling; it exists in the play of magic and story-making; it exists in the working of make-believe and game; it exists as joy in every form of dancing or singing—and it always seems to exist as some mixture of diverse ingredients. It appears when one least expects it, in fact, which may say at least something about what it is. One of Conrad Hyers' several books on comedy and the Christian faith provides an exhaustive discussion of the gamut of comedic forms, focusing on the range of comic "types"—the humorist, the jester, the clown, the "child," the simpleton, the underdog, the trickster; all are comedic but all function in strikingly different comedic ways.[7]

Comedy, moreover, tends to be situational; that is, what is funny in one situation may not be funny at all in a different one. What is funny in a given situation at one particular point in time may not be funny in the same situation at some other time. Often, too, it is a common understanding of a given situation that makes a particular action funny; without that common understanding, something that is said or done in front of that particular group of people would not be funny at all. It goes beyond that. Often, it is the symbolically cultivated persona, the comic persona, of an individual that makes a particular action, gesture, or statement funny; someone else doing or saying the same thing would not provoke laughter. For example, Jack Benny carrying a violin onto the stage sets up a comedic situation in which laughs come easily and with few words, whereas someone else carrying a violin onto a stage would produce little more than a sense of confusion. Comedy is complicated, and there is no way to simplify it. It is jokes, but it is more than jokes. It is a funny story, but it is more than a funny story. It is Chevy Chase falling down, but it more than that, too. Much more.

Does comedy belong in the Christian pulpit? That depends. It depends, for example, on our developing a well-rounded sense of what comedy is—not an easy thing to do, since there is no one thing that comedy is. It is not so much that Christian theologians who are interested in comedy disagree about it as it is that every theologian—as well as every comedy theorist—has a different take on it. Nor is it easy (or even possible?) to read them all and write something resembling a composite view of, say, theological comedy. There are a few points of agreement; for example, virtually all comedic experts, theological or not, agree that the use of irony plays a large part in what makes something funny; agreement, though, splinters when one gets down to the matter of what makes something comically ironic.

What can be said with certainty is what Harvey Cox said some time ago in a truly sparkling book on the subject:

> For years theologians with a flair for literature have discussed Christianity in relation to the tragic. More recently, however, the tide has begun to turn and we have begun to see an increasing amount of work on Christianity and the comic sensibility. The comic, of course, has to do with more than the funny. It is a perspective on life.[8]

Whether comedy belongs in the pulpit also depends, strangely enough, on the nature of one's theology, something that we shall explore in this book. In fact, it is probably changes in theological currents themselves that have permitted the gradual admission (or readmission) of the comedic into the pulpit. Still, it should be said that the preacher is not, nor should he or she be, a comedian. Few preachers, however funny they are, can match the best of the professional comedians who make us all laugh at some time or other. There is no denying, however, that humor or the comedic, is a part of the pulpit work of a growing number of talented clergy-people. And despite the fact that good comedy, as Cox suggests, does much more than entertain, there is less tendency today to denigrate the entertainment value of a sermon than there was even a generation ago.

Like many others, it is important for me to pay tribute to the liberating influence of Prof. Fred B. Craddock, whose sermons stand at the heart of this study, and with whom it was my privilege to study for two years. Throughout the book, references will be made to Craddock's sermon "When the Roll Is Called Down Here," which is reprinted in the Appendix, with his permission. It is no secret that at the heart of his renown as a preacher is the remarkable way in which he makes us all laugh. He opened the comedic doors for many of us. Yet, while his sermons and even his workshops are filled with humor, he has written remarkably little about the subject. He did argue for its use early on, in *As One Without Authority*, noting that those who criticize humor in the pulpit are more influenced "by a Puritan heritage than by the Bible." The value of humor for preaching, he added, is that it is a form of "celebration," an expression of fellowship, "a confession of trust in the Creator who made all things as they are and who does not need the protection our humorless piety can afford."[9] Preaching as celebration: that is what has finally begun to dawn on all of us who take to the pulpit. Craddock was among the first homileticians to put his finger on it. Craddock had grown up with Shakespeare, his comedies as well as his tragedies, and he had read Kierkegaard, who a century before his time had connected comedy with Christian faith and experience.[10] In short, Craddock, no reveler he, knew the other side of Comus, the flat-out celebratory side, the comic side, and he invited Comus, with trimmed hair, decent clothes, and a resolute promise to be good, into the pulpit. It is our turn now to become acquainted with that other side of comus. We must do it with care, of course, but the god (God!) of comedy is not dead, not at all. It is, in a sense, the God we all preach.

The study of preaching and comedy that follows here is in three parts; and while the reader will most likely be anxious to get to the second part, the first lays important groundwork. Part I represents an effort, in a sense, to clear the air about the relationship between comedy and preaching. To advocate, as we shall do here, that preaching, whenever possible, should be infused with comic elements is a controversial stance—not for every preacher, to be sure, but certainly for many; and for many who teach preaching. The objections to it are important, as are the responses to those objections. Then there is the relationship, which is not well understood at all, between comedy and theology, particularly the changes that are taking place in theological understanding. Most important, we must begin by making clear what we mean by a comic sermon. It is much more than the usual notion of a few jokes added to an otherwise serious sermon. The reader is urged to proceed through these preliminary matters carefully.

Part II turns to the dynamics that go into the making of the comic sermon. Comedy itself is, as we have already indicated, an extremely complicated matter, and therefore the comic sermon is itself far more complex and difficult than any of us has imagined. But there are things to be learned, and in this study we set those "learning" dimensions out under five headings: the comic story, the comic premise, the comic metaphor, the comic Bible, and the comic persona. The dynamics incorporated under these headings could be broken down in other ways, to be sure; and the reader, after digesting these pages, may be inspired to create new comic forms and possibilities for the preaching process. Finally, Part III turns to making and preaching the comic sermon, offering some practical directives for maximizing one's comic effectiveness in the pulpit. Even here, in the "doing" of the sermon, there are things to be learned by the preacher from those who, in their professional lives, have honed the fine arts of the comedic process.

Part I

Coming to Terms with Comic Preaching

1

The Controversy over Comedy in Preaching

Should the sermon be funny? *Should* the sermon actually encourage laughter? *Should* one preach what we will call a comic sermon? A study of the comic spirit in the pulpit must begin with these questions since their answers are by no means self-evident; and even though this book will answer them in the affirmative, it is important to know that others have contended against the use of the comedic in Christian preaching. The objections, particularly over the course of the twentieth century, have taken four fairly well-defined forms—as objections that we may describe as biblical, as theological, as ethical, and, finally, as rhetorical or practical. We will sketch each of these objections and respond to them as a way of setting up the background for this study of the comic spirit in the pulpit.

First, the biblical objections. They stem largely from the long-held view of the sanctity of the Bible, a view of Bible as the holy word of God, and therefore nothing can be funny about the Bible or its proclamation. Moreover, since the Bible has for centuries been held to be the God-inspired record of real, historical events—events of God coming to earth, moving on earth, God living, dying and rising from the dead, all in the person of Christ—it may be a hopeful story, but it dare not be seen as a funny story. Granted, at a few places in the scriptures, people can be seen laughing at something or other, but laughter is not what characterizes the message of the Bible itself. The *kerygma*, that unique summary of the life, death, and resurrection of Christ, along with the events from which it was fashioned, is dead serious; and the pulpit must so treat it. Sin and forgiveness, suffering and sacrifice, death, redemption, and hope—while these are among the great themes of the Bible, they are not, shall we say, comic themes.[1]

For years, this view of the Bible, emphasizing its utter seriousness, held sway. This view did not, in fact, begin to break down until the latter years of the nineteenth century and extending through the middle of the twentieth century; and it happened indirectly. What changed was the view of the Bible as a clear, historical document, a window, in a sense, on the historical events of the biblical era. With the crumbling of the "historical" point of view (i.e., historical criticism), a new form of biblical criticism, meaning a new view of the Bible, emerged. It was a literary view of the Bible, one well known by now, but one which tried to look not *through* the biblical text to some obscure past reality, but which tried to look squarely *at* the biblical text as a literary creation. The text was understood to be about things "of the past," but it was to be treated as having a verbal life "of its own." When scholars by the mid-twentieth century began "reading" the Bible in that way— as many were doing by the early 1960s—they began to see something they had not seen before. They realized that the biblical documents, *as literary documents,* were, at many points, quite humorous; some even argued that the *stories* that the documents told, if one could get past their "sacredness," were funny as well; and not just funny in the present, but probably very funny for their readers or hearers of the distant past.

Two important and quite different books that helped spark this idea appeared about the same time—in 1964. One was by the eminent Quaker theologian and biblical scholar Elton Trueblood; it was titled *The Humor of Christ.* Few books broke open the question of humor in the New Testament more than this one. Trueblood, always the cautious—he was a Quaker!—but provocative scholar, argued that humor was actually a *strategy* in the teaching of Jesus as we have it in the New Testament. Even now, almost four decades later, Trueblood's discussion of irony as a comedic biblical form has not been surpassed among theologians. What Trueblood wrote as he began that little book can still be said:

> We do not know with certainty how much humor there is in Christ's teachings, but we can be sure that there is far more than is normally recognized. In any case there are numerous passages in the recorded teaching which are practically incomprehensible when regarded as sober prose, but which are luminous once we become liberated from the gratuitous assumption that Christ never joked.[2]

The second book that appeared in 1964 was not itself about humor or comedy in the New Testament; in fact, one can search it in vain for any reference to humor. But it explicitly laid the groundwork out of which others harvested comedic perspectives for the study of the New Testament. The book is Amos Wilder's *Early Christian Rhetoric: The Language of the Gospel*.[3] Wilder proposed that the Christian gospels contain a wide variety of heretofore unappreciated literary genres, specifically nonreligious genres of the biblical era. Those genres were the literary tools for producing all sorts of different responses within those who heard or read them. Wilder's proposal shifted the perspective on the gospel documents enough to cause other scholars to examine them in new ways; and the outcome, which can now be traced, was striking. A number of books immediately followed Wilder, works by scholars such as Dan O. Via, Jr., who focused his studies on the parables.[4] Out of this came a powerful distinction between what he described as parables of tragedy and parables of comedy, a distinction that caught on. The idea of comedy became, in fact, an important new lens through which New Testament scholars came at their texts. Comedy, in other words, emerged—and quickly—as a category for New Testament study. By the mid-1970s, notions of tragedy and comedy as reflective of biblical studies were widespread.

Also influenced by Wilder was another young theologian who added a note of radicality to the emerging discussion of the comedic in the Christian faith. Harvey Cox, though, moved comedy from the gospel genre to the whole of the Christian gospel itself. In his book *The Feast of Fools*, Cox described Christianity itself as comedy and then took it the final steps, describing faith as comic play and naming Christ as the ultimate clown or harlequin. Whereas in previous generations, Cox says, Christ appeared in other guises—as teacher, judge, healer—today such traditional images have lost much of their power. Now, Christ has made an unexpected entrance onto the stage of modern secular life. Enter Christ, Cox says, as the harlequin: the personification of festivity and fantasy in an age that had almost lost both. "Coming now in greasepaint and halo, this Christ is able to touch our jaded modern consciousness as other images of Christ cannot."[5]

It did not take long for all of this to take root homiletically. Frederick Buechner made it, in part, the centerpiece for his Lyman Beecher Lectures in preaching at Yale Divinity School, which were published in 1977 as a widely read little book called *Telling the Truth: The Gospel as Tragedy, Comedy and Fairy Tale*. As Buechner put it at one point:

> I think that these parables can be read as jokes about God in the sense that what they are essentially about is the outlandishness of God who does impossible things with impossible people, and I believe that the comedy of them is not just a device for making the truth that they contain go down easy but that the truth that they contain can itself be thought of as comic.[6]

The point is that while it probably cannot be called a consensus, it is fair to say that the old biblical objections to comedy in preaching can no longer be sustained very well. The Bible is no longer seen as a somber, sober, heavy document; nor is the faith that it embodies. Moreover, fresh, interesting biblical studies of the sort that Trueblood did with Christ's humor still appear from time to time—witness Douglas Adams' *The Prostitute in the Family Tree: Discovering Humor and Irony in the Bible*, published in 1997 as a notable recent example.[7] Why, then, can the preaching of the Bible not reflect that? The answer is that it not only can, but it should.

Objections Theological

The second set of objections to comedy in the pulpit are *theological*, as distinct from specifically biblical ones. While many theologians—Karl Barth chief among them—have merely passed over the entire subject of humor as their way of objecting to it, some have made theological cases against comic elements as far as faith and preaching are concerned. For the most part, these are neo-orthodox theologians, working in that tradition which has exerted such a profound influence throughout the twentieth century. It is, moreover, neo-orthodox theology—which we will examine more carefully in the next chapter—that has argued, as it still does, against the comic spirit as part of the spirit of Christian preaching. Probably the most widely read and influential statement about comedy from the neo-orthodox vantage point was that of Reinhold Niebuhr, which first appeared in his 1946 book *Discerning the Signs of the Times* and which was reprinted more than twenty years later in Conrad Hyers' book *Holy Laughter*.

In that essay, Niebuhr described a clear relationship between Christian faith and humor, "derived from the fact that both deal with the incongruities of our existence." But then he made his crucial distinction: "Humor is concerned with the immediate incongruities of life and faith with the ultimate ones." So, "laughter is our reaction to the immediate incongruities and those which do not affect us essentially. Faith is the only possible response to the ultimate incongruities of existence which threaten the very meaning of our life." From that, then, Niebuhr draws his widely quoted conclusion:

> Insofar as the sense of humor is a recognition of incongruity, it is more profound than any philosophy which seeks to devour incongruity in reason. But the sense of humor remains healthy only when it deals with immediate issues and faces the obvious and surface irrationalities. It must move toward faith or sink into despair when the ultimate issues are raised. That is why there is laughter in the vestibule of the temple, the echo of laughter in the temple itself, but only faith and prayer, and no laughter, in the holy of holies."[8]

Implicit in this is also an ethical objection to humor surrounding ultimate things, which we will take up in a moment. His theological argument, though, is based on a firm distinction between what he calls immediate realities and ultimate ones, between life lived in an immediate world and a world of faith. The line that divides those worlds, Niebuhr says, is the line that can be drawn around the pulpit, the "holy place" where the word of God is preached. Humans can and do laugh about the irrationalities and incongruities of living, and it is that laughter which may "echo in the temple"; but one cannot laugh about the ultimates of faith and worship, about sin and forgiveness, those matters that are taken up, finally, at the altar of God, at the pulpit or the table in the "holy of holies." Countless preachers over the past fifty years have heeded Niebuhr's call for a ban on laughter in the sermon.

Are there other theological ways, though, to assess the nature of humor as it relates to the most sacred spaces of the church? The answer is yes. While the range of theologians who have affirmed humor in some degree over the past few decades is far beyond the scope of this brief chapter, a few have given the subject considerable attention in their theological work.

One is Conrad Hyers, who has devoted his theological life, as it were, to the study of the comic in all its myriad forms. His book *Holy Laughter* has become the classic set of essays on the subject, and his own contributions at the opening and close of it are among its best. Moreover, he has continued to write about theology and humor over the years with both insight and thoroughness. Hyers' perspective is that whether one is talking about liturgy, the nature of God, human nature, or the Bible, the line between the sacred and the secular no longer exists, if it ever did. There is no longer a holy of holies; or, if there is, it is not in the place where we have long assumed it to be. The sacred and the secular (or profane) are not just a difficult blend; they often switch places and identities completely. For Hyers, comedy, by its nature, is disruptive, and particularly disruptive of those things upon which ultimate seriousness is conferred. This is because humor, by its nature, does not take the sacred with "unqualified seriousness," nor does it "absolutize" holy things. In fact, Hyers argues, humor actually works to annul the distinction between the holy and the unholy; it wants to tear down the veil between the mundane, "immediate" world and the holy of holies. Humor, in fact, wants to claim that *it* is the rightful heir of the holy of holies. As Hyers puts it, "Far from humor being a sign of the fall of man, and a trespass upon the holy ground of the sacred, the absense of humor and the loss of the comic perspective signifies the pride symbolized by the fall, and comedy a reminder of paradise-lost."[9]

For Hyers, when the wall between the world and temple, between the sacred and the profane, is removed, a new frontier of faith is actually created, the place where laughter reigns, but the laughter that is heard is holy laughter. Humor, in fact, lies squarely on that holy frontier between the sacred and the profane; it may be understood as an "interlude, half-playful, half-serious, which takes place in a zone between the sacred and the profane, and which has its own validity within the religious encounter."[10] Faith itself becomes an element of play, and thus of laughter. The unholy becomes holy in that kind of play; the holy becomes unholy. The universe itself laughs at the fun of it all.

The issue that occupies Hyers is not whether laughter belongs in the pulpit, or in the holy of holies; it is the question, instead, of what makes laughter holy. For Hyers, the answer is summed up in distinguishing between humor as profanation and humor as profanity.[11] Holy laughter is not profanity, but it is often profanation. Profanation is the ability to laugh at things understood to be holy or revered, but that are flawed and human nonetheless. For laughter to be holy, Hyers contends, the things laughed at must be held in utter seriousness. It sounds like a contradiction, but it is not; instead, it ranks as a paradox of profoundest importance. We take ourselves seriously, very seriously, so we can laugh at ourselves; and it is a holy laughter. When we take our leaders seriously, whether political or religious, we can laugh at them; and it is a holy laughter. When we take our system of governance seriously, then we can laugh at those who lead it and work in it; and it is a holy laughter. When we take our religious faith seriously, then we can laugh at our efforts in it; and it is a holy laughter.

By the same token, laughter turns into profanity when those who laugh do so at things that they do not take seriously. It is then that the laughter turns to mockery, to cynicism, hollowness, and even hatred. It is the laughter of the crowd at Jesus' crucifixion. It is the laughter of derision directed by one group at those who are held to be inferior. It is the laughter of the racist as cruelty is meted out against a helpless victim of another race. It is the laughter that arises, at its root, from the dehumanization of others, a vicious and ugly laughter. That unholy laughter stands at odds with laughter that is holy, holy by virtue of the fact that it first humanizes, and in that humanization sees and embraces all the patterns of shared human frailty. That is the difference between holy and unholy laughter. Moreover, Hyers rejects Niebuhr's distinction between laughter as appropriate when directed at immediate human things but inappropriate before ultimate faith matters. For Hyers, any laughter is appropriate when it takes human life seriously, with all of its flaws. That is holy laughter; and Hyers believes that it not only can be admitted to the holy of holies; it probably finds its greatest expression there. He also wants to go a step beyond that, though, to say that wherever "holy laughter" takes place, there the holy of holies itself exists.

Other Responses to Niebuhr

Two other theological perspectives on the comic have been very influential; both, to a certain extent, are responses to the mandate given by Niebuhr. One is the perspective of Peter Berger, the theologian and sociologist. For Berger, humor is at the heart of the Christian idea of transcendence. "Comedy," Berger writes, is not transcendence itself, but "is a signal, an intimation, of transcendence."[12] The language of transcendence here must be clarified, however, since later (in the next chapter) the word will appear again. Here, Berger's language of transcendence does not refer to the position of God vis-à-vis humankind; that is, God as a "transcendent" God. For Berger, transcendence refers to a human capacity, an ability that enables the human being to rise above or transcend the circumstances of life and humanness; and laughter becomes the means by which this transcendence is achieved. If one perceives of the human condition as a kind of prison in which we are all cosmically held, then tragedy—or what Berger calls "tragic catharsis"—is what makes us "look upon the greatness man is capable of even within this finitude and prepares us to accept the human condition." On the other hand, comedy's role— the "comic catharsis"—presents us with "a fleeting image of man transcending his finitude and, if only for a brief moment, gives us the exhilarating idea that perhaps it will be man, after all, who will be the victor in the struggle in a universe bent on crushing him."[13] Berger connects this directly to the Christian faith, saying that in a way strangely parallel to Christianity

> comedy overcomes the tragic perspective. From the Christian point of view, one can say that comedy, unlike tragedy, bears within it a great secret. This secret is the promise of redemption. For redemption promises in eternity what comedy gives us in its few moments of precarious liberation— the collapse of the walls of our imprisonment.[14]

The other important theologian of the comic is one to whom we have already referred. He is Harvey Cox, whose book *The Feast of Fools* locates comedy in a larger framework of the postmodern problem of believing, of Christian belief itself. There is nothing to believe in anymore, he says. We are no longer interested even in doubting. It is all just irrelevant. The world of faith not only has come apart; it has given way to a world of nihilistic violence, debased values, and lostness. The only possible way out, Cox argues—or argued a few decades ago—is pointed to by the coming of the harlequin Christ, the comic Christ. We must, with this laughing Christ, learn the laugh of affirmation. It is that laughter which gives new life to the very idea of praying. "Our ability to laugh while praying is an invaluable gift," he writes; something that "is not understood by sober believers or by the even more sober athiests among us."[15]

We can, of course, laugh the dark laugh of nervousness and fear, the laugh of nihilism, the laugh that arises when one senses that there is nothing left at all, so we might as well laugh at our weird predicament. Or, Cox says, we can find in the spirit and practice of laughter itself the kind of play that becomes a way to reframe life and belief. Laughter, play, in this sense becomes the affirmation. The clown affirms by denying: "But in denying he is also affirming. He enables us to laugh at our successes and failures, at our fears and our faith. By involving us in his denial he lures us into affirming after all." Laughter, in this sense, becomes the new voice of faith. It is, as Cox puts it, the expression "not only of our ironic confidence and our strange joy, but also of our recognition that there is no 'factual' basis for either."[16] In desperate times, such as these are, when nothing is secure and chance seems fully and even destructively in control, there is only what Cox calls comic hope left. It is this kind of "irrepressible radical hope" that is kept alive and well today in the comic. Wherever there is true laughter, the laughter of human beings remembering good times and toasting joyous occasions, the laughter of filling a room with jesting and wild imagining, one is searching for hope. Moreover, as Cox puts it, laughter is "hope's last weapon." When we face disaster and death, "we laugh instead of crossing ourselves. Or, perhaps better stated, our laughter is a way of crossing ourselves. It shows that despite the disappearance of any empirical basis for hope, we have not stopped hoping."[17]

While we have only scratched the surface here, it is clear that a number of important and credible theologians have thought deeply about the theological implications of comedy—theologians who are not only willing to *admit* humor into the holy of holies, but who believe that without humor, without laughter, *there is no holy of holies*. While these theologians come at the subject in different ways with different emphases and arguments, they all affirm the unique nature of laughter—Hyers as a humanizing agent,

Berger as a sign of redemptive human transcendence, and Cox as the essence of hope in a hopeless world.

Objections Ethical

We must turn to a third set of objections to comedy in the pulpit, though. These are the ethical objections. It is Niebuhr again who has given most sensitive voice to this perspective. He wrote:

> Laughter may turn to bitterness when it faces serious evil, partly because it senses its impotence. But, in any case, serious evil must be seriously dealt with. The bitterness of derision is serious enough; but where is the resource of forgiveness to come from? It was present in the original forebearance of laughter; but it can not be brought back into the bitterness of derision. The contradiction between judgment and mercy cannot be resolved by humour but only by vicarious pain.[18]

Laughter, Niebuhr argues, is not an appropriate response to human evil, the evil of oppression, war, hunger, and the numerous other scourges of human power. It is certainly true that serious evil must be dealt with seriously; the role of vicarious pain, the role of sacrifice and solidarity with victims, cannot be minimized. It is also true that laughter, when it turns to bitterness, does reflect an impotence that is self-defeating at best. But if one thinks back over the theological perspectives of Hyers, Berger, and Cox, one finds clear, if implicit, responses to the ethical concern of Niebuhr. There is, of course, the horrid laughter of the oppressor; there is also the equally appalling laughter of those on the sidelines who laugh at what they take to be their superiority over the oppressed. These are forms of demonic laughter—which is Hyers' point. But there is also the laughter—or should be the laughter—of the oppressed and those who would work to free them. This is the laughter that keeps them human in the most inhuman of circumstances.

Here Berger picks up the strain. We indicated earlier that, for Berger, the comic is the key to what he calls transcendence. But transcendence has two dimensions for Berger, and so far we have only taken account of one of them—the one in which the comic produces the transcendence by which one rises above the human condition, a kind of cosmic transcendence. For Berger, however, there is another important dimension in which comedy serves transcendence. This one refers to the condition of countless peoples of the past and present who find themselves in various kinds of oppression, in *real* prisons of human making. Here, too, comedy plays its transcending role. Laughter, of course, is no substitute for actual liberation, but laughter plays a crucial role in keeping the human spirit alive and assured that walls can be climbed. Laughter becomes what Berger calls a "living defiance," not only of the laws of nature, but of the "laws of man." Laughter enables the human spirit to "defy gravity and the resistance of matter." Through laughter, the spirit stays kindled when by every law and logic it should go out. With laughter, one finds solidarity with other laughing souls who share the struggle for release from whatever the confinement is. There is the laughter of human defiance, the full bore of humanity exerting itself in the face of who-knows-what. There is the laughter of resistance, the laughter that wells up out of the human depth itself.[19]

Cox picks it up, too, with ethical notions clearly in mind. There is the laughter of hope, the laughter of a hope for hope, the laughter of remembering mingled with conjuring up another future, somehow, somewhere. There is the laughter that is an all-out cry to God, a laughter that refuses, against all odds, to ever give up. Of course there can be laughters of bitterness and impotence; but mixed with those laughters is the faint glow of hope against hope. From these points of view, the comic spirit is not some "giving in" to injustice and oppression. Instead, the comic spirit leads to *more, not less*, participation in the struggle for justice and humanness in a world where the sound of laughter dare not be extinguished.

The Practical Objections

We turn, though, to the fourth type of objection to comedy in the pulpit, the kind that we may characterize as rhetorical or practical. This objection takes at least three different forms, though others could surely be described as well. The first is the one that objects—and rightly so—to the use of jokes in the pulpit. This book, too, shall argue against the use of jokes in preaching. Jokes, however well told, are distracting and often annoying, whenever and wherever they are told, but particularly in sermons; and very few people, including preachers, are naturally good at telling jokes. Jokes should not be used to "introduce" a sermon, because they seldom provide anything introductory. They should not be used to "warm up" an audience or congregation before the sermon begins, since jokes invariably fall flat and one must hope that the sermon itself can warm up a congregation after the chill of a joke gone bad.

Often homileticians take stands against comedy or humor in preaching when what they are really taking a stand against is the use of jokes in the sermon. But the two things should not be equated. Jokes are only one form of humor, and a very small form at that. Once a year, Garrison Keillor devotes a *Prairie Home Companion* radio broadcast to what he calls "joke night"; it amounts to two nonstop hours of jokes, most of them dumb jokes that actually parody the joke. But that is only once a year. The remaining two dozen or so *Prairie Home Companion* broadcasts on public radio each year are also deeply and creatively humorous, filled with warmth and laughter, but all based on the myriad other forms of the comedic and all decidedly *not* dependent on the joke. One can readily argue against the use of jokes in sermons for numerous reasons, but this does not mean that, in doing so, one is arguing against the comic spirit being utilized in the sermon.

A second practical or rhetorical objection to humor in preaching is based on the relationship between humor and sarcasm. As David Buttrick has pointed out in his book *Homiletic*, while sarcasm can certainly produce laughter, it is a destructive laughter that can devastate preaching.[20] Sarcasm is invariably hostile and based on hatred, whatever form that hatred takes, against whatever it is directed, or however veiled it might be. But the danger is a very real one as far as the sermon is concerned, since the preacher can easily lapse into it, sometimes under the guise of being forthright or even prophetic.

The overt reaction against sarcasm in preaching from homileticians like Buttrick is more than justified by the history of the American pulpit. This was well documented, though somewhat inadvertently, by Douglas Adams (to whose 1997 book we referred earlier) in his 1975 doctoral dissertation, titled *Humor in the American Pulpit: From George Whitefield through Henry Ward Beecher*, a study of eighteenth- and nineteenth-century preaching. What Adams caught was that the humor of even the great preachers of that pre-industrial era in America was based almost exclusively on sarcasm and ridicule, directed invariably at the "infidels" of the age, both as individuals and as the collective perpetrators of the age's untold "idolatries." The mood of the humor is captured in a story told of Henry Ward Beecher who, when he was in the midst of an impassioned sermon, was interrupted by a drunken man in the balcony who began waving his arms and crowing like a rooster. Instantly, Beecher stopped, took out his watch, and remarked: "What—morning already? I wouldn't have believed it, but the instincts of the lower animal are infallible."[21]

Such attitude and language, humorous or not, have no place in the contemporary pulpit, however they might have been viewed one hundred and fifty years ago. Like the joke, they must be banned from preaching; but just as the joke cannot be equated with a full expression of the comic spirit, neither can sarcasm or ridicule be. The comic spirit does not need sarcasm or ridicule, however they might have existed in preaching in ages past; moreover, the comic spirit can flourish in the pulpit quite well without such deadly humorous forms.

A third rhetorical or practical objection to comedy or humor in the sermon is quite different from the first two. It has to do with the understanding that in humor there is power, considerable power. This power lies in the ability to cause people to laugh. As one astute homiletician put it, he dislikes humor in the pulpit because—and he speaks from the viewpoint of one in the pew—it can be used to "persuade me for or against an opinion."[22] The implication is that when people laugh, their intellectual and psychic defenses are lowered or removed and they become susceptible to influences against which, without the laughter, they would be able to "protect" themselves. This is a fairly common suspicion about laughter, about the comedic: that it is somehow subversive; that when we laugh, we become vulnerable in ways that we are not when we are not "forced" to laugh. This viewpoint is related to various ideas about modern advertising, that is, that comedy sells products better than serious pitches. What most advertising research shows, though, is that people do, in fact, like to laugh and tend to look favorably on situations that "permit" them to laugh; and if certain products—not all of them, it should be said—are associated with comedy and laughter, those products also may be favorably perceived.

What is *not* true, however—much to the chagrin of the advertising industry—is that people cease to be thinking, reflective human beings when they are made to laugh. Humor does not negate the critical faculties, putting them, as it were, on hold until the laughter stops—which is what the comment above suggests. The contrary is actually the case, as we shall see in more detail in a later chapter. Laughter tends to be a profound method for building critical sensibility and discernment, not just intellectually but, more important, holistically, since it also involves intuitions and emotions in the complex comedic mixture. There is the power of the ironic, of the skewed observation, that makes us laugh; and our laughter arises because we are confronted with a new way of seeing something. There is the power of the unexpected twist on a story that provokes laughter because we are pressed to confront something we have been reluctant to deal with. There is the power of the funny anecdote that makes us laugh in a recognition of something we know to be true but that has been hidden, in a sense, from us.

But it is still more complex than that. The power of the comic story, with the emphasis now on the word "story," is for many a frightening power, one that the sermon must not embrace. Its power is one of inclusion and exclusion, quite apart from concerns with sarcasm and ridicule. By their very nature, stories have parameters: it is what makes them stories. And the setting of those parameters can both include and exclude, including those who can identify with the story while excluding those who cannot. In this book, we shall take full account of this problem in the comic story, specifically considering ways of not falling prey to it or, at least, of minimizing it as a problem for the sermon. What should be said at this point is that the creative power of the comic story correctly understood and used in a sermon far outweighs the potential dangers that lurk in a haphazard use of the story.

There are, no doubt, other objections that one can read or even discover from one's own experience with comic elements in the pulpit; most of them derive, though, from what we have briefly looked at here. It is true that while all of us love to laugh, not all laughter is good, nor should all of the ways in which laughter is produced be condoned, let alone brought to the pulpit. In preaching, it is never acceptable to induce laughter for the sake of laughter. It is never acceptable, either, to prompt laughter for the sake of winning acceptance from one's congregants or for hoping that in their laughter one's congregants will like the preacher more than they otherwise would. Laughter is not a gimmick, and when it deteriorates into one—or when the preacher seeks to use it as one—then that laughter overwhelms the gospel, and preaching degenerates into something not fit for the pulpit. But, properly understood and skillfully used, the comic spirit, and the laughter that can arise from it, is one of those elements that can lift a mediocre pulpit to the level of greatness.

Can there be laughter in the holy of holies? *Should* there be laughter there? Not only can there be—there ought to be. In the concluding essay of Hyers' book *Holy Laughter*, theologian Chad Walsh says that a "great part of the malaise afflicting Christianity today, particularly in its Protestant forms, is that it has forgotten (or never learned) how to laugh. Like Niebuhr, he adds, "it fails to realize that even (maybe especially) in the holy of holies (people) are set free by the ultimate presence of God so that in that fellowship they can offer whatever gifts they come bearing, including the gift of humor."[23]

2

The Resurgence of Comedy
in Preaching

If, as a growing number of scholars now suggest, the comic spirit infused the character and words of the Jesus stories in the New Testament, then where did that comic spirit go for so many intervening years between then and now? Why is it possible for us to talk about a resurgence or a reappearance of the comic spirit within Christianity in recent times? Harvey Cox puzzled over such questions some years ago in his book *The Feast of Fools*. He argued that the symbol of Christ as a clown-like figure, as a full-blown religious harlequin, was right for that early era of religious confrontation. The Christ-figure, with crown and scepter of thorns and wood, who could be exalted to his "throne" only after his humiliating defeat, was a remarkable exercise in parody and irony, the stuff of which comedy is fashioned.

But then things changed. The church emerged and took on the trappings not of parodied power, but of real power. The thorns and wood turned into real gold and real jewels. In place of the commoner's garb worn by Jesus, it took on its own royal finery. The ridiculous image of Christ the Clown gave way to a sublime and unsmiling hierarchy. So the Church was during most of the long years of its history. Cox contended that the comic spirit did not die out of Christianity altogether, however, but that it persisted here and there as a sort of underground movement, with the medieval street skits and morality plays, for example. But overall the comic spirit disappeared, since, as Cox put it, "What place is there for caricature when the church's regal vestments are taken seriously?"

Now, though—Cox was reflecting the mood of the late 1960s and early 1970s—the comic spirit of Christianity in our secularized, postmodern era is beginning to reemerge. In the arts of the twentieth century, for example, we had the first glimmerings of a new appreciation of a clownish Christ. We are once again beginning to embrace the harlequin at the center of faith. We are rediscovering the humor that permeates the New Testament. Laughter is again new to the church after centuries of being banned from it. In retrospect, we can see Reinhold Niebuhr's statement in a different light with this resurgence in mind. Niebuhr was, in fact, willing to admit humor and laughter into the church, if they were confined to the vestibule, and if only their echo was actually heard in the temple itself. But, at mid-century when Niebuhr wrote, that was itself an awareness, however dim, that something was happening. Even Niebuhr was willing, in a sense, to allow laughter halfway into the church, an important step, no doubt, in what would be its invitation back into the holy of holies itself— where Christ the Clown holds forth.

Cox did not, however, explore the question of why this remarkable change in the past few decades has come about. As he suggested, though, the answer to that has to arise from the larger social and cultural shifts of the recent past, and from the relationship between those shifts and changes in theology itself. Cox's suggestion, and the one that concerns us in this chapter, is that the resurgence of the comic spirit as a part of contemporary theology—and with it contemporary preaching—is not coincidental. Nor is it just a result of secularization, or of some breakdown in either culture or theology. It has resulted, we may contend, from a kind of intellectual alliance between comedy and new forms of theological thinking, forms that are associated with what we generally know as postmodern theology. But, to explain this, we must take it a step at a time—first with some notes on the definition of classic comedy, followed by a sense of the new postmodern theologies themselves. What we will find is a convergence of sorts, resulting from a recent transition from orthodox theologies that were intellectually inhospitable to comedy to new theologies that not only are intellectually compatible with it, but that virtually foster the comic spirit.

The Struggle for Definition

We begin, then, by devising a definitional framework for understanding comedy, not a definition per se, since that may be something of an impossibility, but a framework out of which the comedic invariably arises. The comic spirit has at least five major dimensions which we may summarize here from a wide variety of comedic theories. They are: (1) its immanence, or the clear and unrelenting focus of comedy on human relationship as the essence of all life and being; (2) its doubting, or its deliberate drive to question everything; (3) its incongruity, or its wavering focus on the disparities present in all human life and interaction—in other words, its fundamental irony; (4) its drive to create and sustain ambiguity; and (5), suprisingly, its underlying goal of promoting human, or social, equality and solidarity. We should look at each of these briefly.

The first dimension of the comedic is its immanence. Some scholars of comedy have called attention to a fundamental distinction between the tragic spirit and the comic one. It is that the tragic spirit, whether it takes form in a play, in a myth, or in some work of visual art, is invariably an other-worldly spirit. The processes of life, thought, and ultimately control over all things human are lodged in some other sphere; and while that other world impacts the human living of life, the true center of things is thought to be in that separate, one might say transcendent, domain. In other words, this view assumes two worlds, this one and that one, with *that* one, the cosmic other world, holding sway over the affairs of this one.

The great social theorist of comedy Hugh Dalziel Duncan has argued that this is the reason that over the centuries Christianity has been a tragic religion instead of a comic one.[1] It has been an other-worldly religion. Some Christians today would argue with Duncan's characterization of Christianity as essentially "tragic"— and thus having little place for anything comic. Some will want to say that the "resurrection" of Christ negates the tragic vision, turning it into a joyful motif. The gospel, they point out, means that while we might have been "born in sin," we are now "saved," and that is the good news of the Christian religion. The fact is, though, that such a theological motif or emphasis on the "joy of salvation" is itself remarkably recent, and may not yet even represent the core or the mainstream of either Protestant or Catholic theology. One may easily argue that the resurgence of the comic in Christian theology in the second half of the twentieth century has itself forced theologians to think about a "joyful" gospel, a comic one, rather than a gospel that maintains a crucifix as its centerpiece.

The comic spirit, on the other hand, instead of being other-worldly, is profoundly of "this world," immanent. It is a worldly spirit that focuses unrelentingly on the processes and problems of human relation and ethic, one that believes in the human ability, if not to solve all human problems, at least to confront them and live with them. Comedy, that is, arises from the interplay of human beings, from the gaffes and foibles of humans trying not only to cope with each other, but with themselves. We laugh at seeing the high brought low, at seeing the gap between ideal and actual, at reenactments of our best efforts to achieve goals that have been thwarted again and again, goals that we somehow know may never be achieved. We are who we are, by ourselves and together, and in our mundane dealings we absorb whatever hurts come our way and strive for new heights, usually unsuccessfully, through laughter. After all, what we have is all we can be sure of; and we are not really sure of that.

Great comic artists, in Duncan's words, "do not believe that salvation can be achieved by controlling forces outside" of human reach, "either in 'Society,' 'Nature,' or 'God'—but only in the struggle of [humans] to communicate in love and hate."[2] From the comedic point of view, human beings must confront as openly and candidly as they can the miseries of life and, in Duncan's words, keep staring them in the face. Only by doing so, the comic spirit says, is there any ultimate hope of controlling those miseries. As Duncan puts it, "Only so long as we keep our minds flexible and alive in discussion, talk, and laughter do we survive as human beings."[3] That is the comic spirit.

The contrast between the tragic and comic spirits can be extended, underscoring even further the transcendent emphasis of tragedy and the immanent emphasis of comedy. Both comedy and tragedy are purgative, providing humans with release from guilt or from the grasp of evil. Tragedy purges through the sacrifice of victims who have been selected and prepared by the gods in what amounts to a vicarious atonement for those who participate in the sacrifice. Comedy, on the other hand, is also purgative, but in a very different way. Its "victims" are not "from above," but arise from among the people themselves. But those victims are not expected to die in a sacrificial rite; in fact, one does not wish to see them die. Comic victims are the clowns who "suffer" ridicule or degradation, who can be hammered again and again in a non-lethal way; and the purgation is carried out in the rites of laughter directed at those who, in effect, take such "hammering" upon themselves. Hence, the universal comedy of poking and punching, of malleting, of taking terrible falls, of having heavy objects land on one's feet, or getting a pie in the face—all are what we consider the interactions of slapstick.

Moreover, the "authority" for *tragic* rites of expiation is, again, other-worldly. What is good and what is evil and the punishments for violating the good-evil principles, are determined above and beyond this world in which mere mortals move. That is what traditional forms of religion and ethics are all about. In *comedy*, however, the "authority" for the rites of expiatory laughter is derived from human society or culture itself, from people who gather and designate the clown, that pathetic and odd figure upon which their feelings of hopelessness and helplessness can be heaped. As for good and evil, that, too, is recognized in comedy as a collective social agreement, and it is the clown who points out the violations of both. It is, in fact, that "pointing out" from which the comic spirit arises.

The immanence of the comic spirit is also visible in the ways in which tragedy and comedy view heroes and villains. At the heart of the disparity is that in tragedy the hero must die for the "sinners," the villains; only by doing so can the hero save those who cannot save themselves. The hero comes "from the gods" and often is one; but "god" must die for the masses. In the comic mode, however, it is not that way. The "hero"—again the clown—must suffer, but in that suffering the clown must not, indeed cannot, die. If the clown dies, the people die. The clown is perpetually down, perpetually assaulted; and, in that, the clown becomes the symbol of the battering of the people themselves. But the clown, despite the suffering and the battering, does not die. As long as the clown bounces back, the people know that they, too, will bounce back. The clown absorbs the punishment, but is forever resilient; the clown, shall we say, always "rises again." It is a kind of perpetual resurrection, but one without death. It is a merging of resurrection and laughter; and the people who see it, who participate in it, understand and share both the resurrection and the laughter.

In this, the clown and the people merge. They "know each other." The clown is one of them. The clown represents them. The clown will be laughed at, again and again; but the clown is always being laughed with. The clown is creating the laughter and absorbing all of the feelings that go with the collective laughter. We laugh to purge the clown, and hence ourselves, of folly, stupidity, greed, and malice. It is not that the clown does for the people what they cannot do for themselves, as in tragedy; but in the actions of the clown the people are doing what only they can do for themselves.

Institutionalized Doubt

The second dimension of the comedic spirit is a deliberate and unrelenting sense of doubt. The comic is one who questions everything, who asks the naive questions "Why?" "How?" or "Who says?" In the tragic orientation, doubting is, for all practical purposes, prohibited. To doubt is to undermine; it is to tear down. In the tragic, doubting is the road to heresy and detachment from legitimate authorities. In the comic perspective, however, the opposite is the case. Doubting is considered the road to truth, or at least as close to truth as humankind can ever attain. In fact, in comedy the process of seeing things in a constantly questioning, constantly challenging, mode is the ultimate value. It is the value that keeps reason fresh and discourse flexible and viable. In doubting, the comedian constantly detaches himself or herself, along with the audience, from a social order's "sacred beliefs." This is not done to debunk those beliefs, but to keep them always open to evaluation and modification. In fact, the assumption is that in order for beliefs or behaviors or motives or values to be challenged by the comic, everyone involved, the comic included, must take those beliefs, behaviors, motives, or values *seriously*. The comedian, in short, does not reject authority, but uses doubt and questioning to open up authority—all authority, whether secular or religious—to perpetual scrutiny.

Duncan demonstrates, in fact, that comedy actually "institutionalizes" doubt and questioning. One recognizes the jester, an official of the "court," the one whose "job" it is to satirize or poke fun at the formalities or the rules or even at those who trumpet the formalities and make the rules. It becomes what, in an open society, one might see as "sanctioned disrespect." The king, as Duncan says, is burlesqued. The queen is satirized. The actions and demeanors of those in authority are questioned, are held up for close and even exaggerated examination, and thus for laughter. Even the king and queen are called on to laugh. It is serious laughter, a laughter related to that which results from the forbidden being broached. In such sanctioned questioning, probing, pushing, pulling, and holding things up for ribbing, the gods are humanized and the priestly rites demystified.

The third dimension of the comic spirit is an irrepressible exploration of the incongruities of our lives. This is the comedy created when disparities or even conflicts within an individual or social order are made explicit and held up for public scrutiny. Such disparities are everywhere, among classes and situations of people, between institutions and the needs of people, between social ends and means, between our ideals and our actions, and between what we pretend to be and what we know we are. It is the comic who raises these discrepancies or incongruities to full consciousness, the consciousness from which laughter can and invariably does arise. Again, when such disparities or incongruities are held up by the clown or the comic there is a measure of safety or legitimacy in what might otherwise be disrespectful or offensive and thereby subject to reprisals.

Most often, the problem that we humans have with the incongruities that plague us is our lack of awareness of them. They are, by and large, hidden from us, whether consciously or unconsciously. Thus, the jolt of the comic who forces us to look at the hidden. We think we are one way, but the comic shows us another aspect of ourselves, one incongruent with what we think we are or are like. We are "hit" with the truth. When we are confronted with our own "contradictions" or the contradictions around us, they strike us as funny, often riotously funny. They seem funny to us, though—and not mortifyingly embarrassing—because we are given a sense of distance from the discrepancies, the incongruities, of our lives by the comic setting itself. The usual, or expected, reactions are suspended, and we are free to respond with laughter at the very idea that we could be so weirdly incongruous. It is the comedian, and the comic situation, that gives us that distance.

Duncan points out that such human incongruities are at the heart of all classic comedy, from George Bernard Shaw and Oscar Wilde to the operettas of Gilbert and Sullivan. As a theme from Gilbert and Sullivan puts it, things are seldom what they seem; skim milk masquerades as cream. The prince is really a commoner; the commoner, we learn in the end, is really the prince. The babies were switched at birth. The formal is actually very silly when the comic makes us look at it closely. The silliness is ritualized to the point of absurd predictability and formality. The moment of enjoyment, of laughter, derives from a sudden awareness, an instant of clarification of a particular incongruity. The prisoner was really free all the time, while the guard was the incarcerated one. The person who appeared to be morally pure had a heart full of lust. The shabby down-and-outer had the IQ of a genius. The most intelligent person of all, when it came right down to it, was the child or the uneducated fool. It was, after all, the child who cried out that the emperor was naked, something that everyone else saw, but would not see. It is the incongruity of men in tuxedos and women in ballroom gowns tumbling one by one into a swimming pool, the incongruity of Red Skelton's Freddy the Freeloader fastidiously setting a table for lunch with flowers and cloth, but doing so with scraps plucked from garbage, set on a table made from a door propped up on two oil drums.

So the comic creates a routine by focusing on the religious evangelist who makes headlines in photographs with a prostitute. There is pain in it, but there is undeniable comedy as well. The comedy is in the sheer incongruity. Things are seldom what they seem. The comic creates a routine by talking about a church that "stands for" a gospel of sacrifice and poverty in a building with a million dollars worth of stained glass windows. The comedy is in the incongruity. The comic pokes fun, we say, but it is fun that in its heart of hearts desires—and places a highest value on—congruity, on honesty. But even here, it is the wide-eyed wonder of the innocent, the child, the simpleton, that opens up to full view the incongruities that are hidden or suppressed because their expression might subject those in power to mockery or disdain. It is the comic as innocent—"what do I know?"—who is given permission, even in official circles, to "expose" the fact of disparity, who can bring it to laughter because of that innocence.

Incongruity as irony is cut from the same cloth. By its nature, irony is two-tiered speech; and in that set of "tiers" is where the incongruity becomes pointedly, and often painfully, clear. One says one thing but, by the nature of how it is said, means something quite different, something that usually stands in stark contrast to the actual words that were spoken. One can lavishly express one's admiration of the president—so lavishly, in fact, that it becomes fully ironic, and the sense of utter dislike is incongruently given powerful form. "Brutus *is* an honorable man." The incongruity is in the saying of one thing and meaning something quite different.

Embracing Ambiguity

Still another dimension of the comic spirit, its fourth, is its embrace of ambiguity. In a world of clearly drawn lines, the comic wants to mess up the lines. The comic believes that the lines are too neat, that things—again—are not what they seem; so we should get rid of the "clear things" if we are going to look in fresh, creative ways at how things are. This is related to incongruity, of course, but it is not the same thing. The comic knows that there is no such thing as a hero or a villain. Such distinctions do not hold up well. Every human being is a mixed bag, part good, part bad, part who-knows-what-in-between. Every human action is also a mixed bag as far as motivation is concerned; whatever it is, the motives behind it are never pure; the lines around "purity" do not draw well at all. The motive is partly good, partly bad, and no one—not even the one who does the act—can ever fully distinguish one from the other.

So, for the comic, the task is to find the places where everything is clear and fixed, where the Christians are neatly separated from the non-Christians, the sheep from the goats, where the saved are weeded out from the mass of unsaved—for the comic, these are the places where one goes to work, as painful as that may sound to many a faithful Christian. In comedy, one focuses on the clear, fixed distinctions, one challenges—doubts—the distinctions and demonstrates, in a sense, the human qualities of good and evil, of struggles and failures, that lie in all of us. So the state's highway commissioner is arrested for speeding—that is not just incongruity, it is also comic ambiguity.

Finally, the goal and end of classic comedy—its fifth dimension—is invariably social equality and solidarity. Both elements are important here. At one level, this means that the high are to be brought low, and those who are low, who are on or near the bottom of the social, political, or economic ladder, are to be lifted up, in a sense; they are to be given respect, dignity, and value. In classic comedic forms, the comic identifies with these lower and middle classes and speaks for them, in a sense, attacking—with laughter—the haughtiness of the proud, the egotistic, the highborn. One aspect of the genius of comedy, in fact, is that it permits the bringing to the surface of hidden, unconscious, subtle—though often brutal—conflict, the conflict, in particular, of classes. One can think about a wide range of classic comedies—from Twain to Molière and George Bernard Shaw to the film comedies of the Marx Brothers, Laurel and Hardy, Chaplin; in all of them a central motif is the disparity of classes, with the comic always at one with those at or near the bottom class. The social hierarchy, moreover, is a problem, one to be attacked always with the hijinks of laughter. Comedy, in short—as Duncan so pointedly notes—is profoundly democratic in spirit. It wants people to live together "in community," not just in harmony, but with an equality that it knows will never be fully achieved but that must ever stand as an ideal.

The comic motive, though, is more complex and probably more realistic than that. It is to pull the lower and middle classes, as it were, *together*, to give them a dignified solidarity as they stand against the upper classes, the oppressing classes. It is based on the idea that, like it or not, "we" at these levels are all in this together. We are, in a sense (whoever "we" are), not alone, regardless of our pains or sufferings. We can laugh together. We can wink at each other in knowing ways in our laughter. We can share our own plight, or our lives, as we laugh at those who, however they do it, stand over us. The comic's job, from this perspective, is not only to let the audience get a good, collective sense of connectedness in laughter; it is also the comic's job to press those who think they are somehow above the common fray to know that they are not. It is more than that, though. It is also that in our laughter our loneliness tends to vanish and we become part of each other. Every comic knows that, as does everyone who comes to relish the comic spirit and situation.

Theologies and Comedy

What we have so far is a kind of definition of comedy, a summary of the characteristics of the comic spirit. While this, in itself, is important to our study, our objective in sketching a definition is to ask the question with which we began this chapter: Why over the past few decades have we seen a resurgence of the comic spirit in both theology and pulpit? Our suggestion (and we will leave it as only a suggestion here) is that the same recent decades have seen the rise of several new and very different forms of Christian theology, theologies that share, in a fairly direct way, the dimensions or characteristics of the comic spirit that we have just outlined. As a result, these recent theologies—the so-called postmodern theologies—not only have room for the comic spirit, but actually embrace it, since the intellectual qualities of that spirit are part and parcel of the intellectual qualities of these new theologies. Let me illustrate by constructing some categories.

First, we said that comedy is an intensely *immanent* art form. That is, it arises from and finds its fullness in complex human relationships and social arrangements. It is a product of human incongruity, whether that incongruity is social, personal, or some mix of the two. Its seminal paradigm is that those who "lord it over others," however they do it, eventually get their comeuppance, and there is delight and laughter when they do. At the root of the comic spirit are the complex relationships that evolve when an individual or group, in biblical language, comes to think more highly of itself than it ought to think. This is the immanence of the comic, which deals in human relationship, interaction, pretense, and unmasking. The point is that when a theology is fundamentally immanent—when God is found and operates, shall we say, in human struggle and relationship—then there exists a theology that, by its nature, not only has room for the immanent comic spirit, but literally invites it. On the other hand, a theology that is fundamentally transcendent or begins with its focus away from humankind in order to "discover" its God in the heavens tends to relinquish the raw materials from which comedy is made; so, as a theology, it has little, if any, place for laughter or the comic spirit.

A second contention concerning comic theory and Christian theology is that theologies that place a premium on well-drawn distinctions and hierarchies between, say, saints and sinners, heroes and villains, do not as a rule tend to be open to the practice of comedy. On the other hand, theologies that embrace a blurring of lines between, say, sin and salvation, good and evil, are theologies that tend not only to value humor but to thrive on it. We are talking about the nature of ambiguity, of course, having noted that ambiguity is one of the marks of the comic sensibility.

Theologically, though, the concept of ambiguity is not an easy one. In some theologies, the word "ambiguity" is used to indicate the mystery of something, of God or of God sending a son in human form to carry out a divine work; there is mystery and uncertainty in how all of that works—and ambiguity is a way often used to talk about those elements. As we have used the term in relation to comedy, however, ambiguity means an end to certainties, a breakdown of neat, careful, easy-to-describe categories. Lines are no longer fixed. Distinctions no longer hold up. Everywhere one looks, things are not what they seem. When theologies embrace ambiguity in this sense, they are open to the comic; when the lines must stay fixed, the comic cannot be embraced.

Third, theologies that find the basis of salvation in some kind of supernatural being or power above, beyond, and apart from human activity are not, by and large, amenable to the comedic. On the other hand, theologies that value the human processes of thinking, reasoning, and, most important, doubting as spiritual exercises, that find their sources of salvation in collective human behavior or activity, are theologies that have a place for humor, for comedy. As Duncan pointed out, the comedic, virtually by definition, is the relentless process of questioning, or doubting, of keeping every option open. The idea is that human beings working together, being together, and, particularly, laughing together—at themselves and their common predicaments—can actually "purge" their common and collective sins. This gives rise to a comedic theological orientation.

Closely related to this is another of Duncan's unique insights. It is that when the purging of sin comes from "above," as it were, it tends to involve human suffering and death. In fact, in such theologies, the dignity of human life itself is said to be found in the act of suffering—in classical Christian doctrine, for example, Christ's suffering and death, and the call to the ideal form of Christian expression through one's own suffering and death for others. Such theologies, one can readily see, have no discernible place for humor. However, when guilt can be purged by the collective activity of the group—say in mythic festivities or in the creation and punishment of clowns or buffoons—then human suffering may be present, but *symbolically* so; and it will not end in death or even in the celebration of dying, but in collective laughter, as in much classical stage comedy. Where there are theologies that embody a sense of the holy within collective human activity itself—not in the summoning of the holy from someplace beyond the collective—then laughter is not only admitted, but it becomes a key part of the collective purging itself.

Finally, since comedy arises from social and economic disparities, from power relationships, only theologies that have an intense concern with such human inequities have room for humor. Duncan pointed out that both tragedy and comedy take evil seriously; but what he then suggested was that tragedy and comedy tend to define evil differently, or at least to locate it in very different places. In tragedy, evil—like God—has a transcendent character. Sin and evil are against God primarily, however they are expressed. Comedy, however, is different; it finds sin and evil primarily within the disparities and oppressions of human society itself. Evil is expressed, in other words, in human misery and mistreatment, in the hold of the powerful over the powerless, and in the unrelenting efforts of the powerless to laugh at and thereby defeat the powerful. Theologies that are deeply involved in life's miseries are theologies that welcome the comedic; it is, in fact, in comedy that those miseries, along with the people who perpetuate them, are mocked via laughter. Theologies that find evil in oppression, in oppressive structures and classes, are theologies that welcome laughter; they need the comedic. Theologies in which evil is related primarily to a transcendent God and only secondarily to the human social condition are not theologies that handle laughter very well, if at all.

Different Kinds of Theologies

There is no desire here to exaggerate or oversimplify what are obviously complex theological issues. Yet it is possible—and very useful—to discern that in what we have sketched above are the roots of two quite different theological orientations. There are what we can describe, for want of a better label, as predominantly transcendent theologies, theologies that find their ultimacy in a God above and beyond all things human, a God who "comes down" from that realm for a time to do for humankind what humankind cannot do for itself. The transcendent theologies easily spin from these central notions to a doctrine of sin as turning away from the transcendent God of the universe, a doctrine that argues that sin issues in death, not only a physical death, but an ultimately spiritual one, a doctrine that God's Son, came to earth to die, literally die, that humankind might not have have to die ultimately; and so on. Such are the essentials of Christian transcendent theologies, even though such theologies have been devised in a multitude of variations. These theologies, moreover, are highly orthodox and neo-orthodox, and have dominated the history of Christian thought and practice from the earliest church formulations until very recently.

As Cox and others have pointed out, the transcendent theologies in their myriad forms have been largely incompatible with the qualities of the comic spirit. It is not at all coincidental that the statements in the previous chapter banning humor or comedy from the church's holy of holies arose from the neo-orthodox tradition of the first half of the twentieth century. This is not to imply anything sinister, as though someone decided that the orthodox or neo-orthodox church could not align itself with the comic spirit. Nothing of the sort happened. Instead, the premises and assumptions of the orthodox, transcendent theologies have simply been incompatible with the premises and assumptions of the comic sensibility. As a result, it could not be admitted to the theological arena.

But that is now changing. Neo-orthodoxy itself has slipped into decline, replaced by the emergence of theologies that virtually for the first time in Christian history challenge the orthodoxies of transcendence. These theological strains have taken hold, though, with remarkable speed. While several such new traditions can be identified, three may be isolated briefly here, not to provide any elaboration of them, but to indicate their underlying commonality. For purposes of definition, we may call these immanent theologies, as opposed to the traditional transcendent ones. Among them are process theology, several strains of narrative theology, and what we may designate as the Jesus theologies.

These are all distinctly this-world theologies, theologies that identify God or the divine not primarily as an other-worldly phenomenon, but as a force that arises from and exists within the complex networks of human interaction and responsibility. Process theology speaks of God, of course, as something quite identifiable, in a sense, but always as an emergent process, the reality of which is shaped by the ongoing searches for the divine within the human heart. Narrative theologies, likewise, while they differ from theologian to theologian, emphasize the presence of God within the "stories" of communities of faith and those who give those communities form and expression. The Jesus theologies, taking their roots from the Gospel stories, find their expression in the human stories, sayings, myths, and legends of Jesus, rather than in the christological formulations of high deity. These theologies tilt, whether their advocates are fully aware of it or not, toward an immanence where the divine takes shape fully within the bosom of the human.

Moreover, these theologies, in varying degrees to be sure, embody other characteristics that are strikingly aligned with those that we have associated with the comedic. For example, these immanent theologies exist by virtue of a desire to "doubt," to challenge how things have always been, how orthodoxy has made its demands. These are theologies that, by their very nature, admire and condone questioning. The human spirit is a questioning spirit, and these are theologies that embrace that very spirit, both implicitly and explicitly. These are also theologies that embrace as well the incongruities of human life, the ambiguities of human life; theologies that are suspicious, often intensely so, of neat, holistic, thoroughly consistent systems of finely wrought doctrine. These are theologies that locate sin and evil not in rebellion against God in a rigorously metaphysical sense, but locate sin and evil in the ways in which human beings treat other human beings. For the most part, too, they locate what orthodoxy would call "redemption" not in the act of a single "god" on earth, but in the actions of human community, then and now.

I do not mean, though, to provide theological exposition here, since these comments are much too brief; I do mean, however, to suggest that when one opens up the fundamental premises and arguments of these new theologies, one finds a striking set of parallels between the characteristics of these new theologies and those of the comic spirit itself. This means, in short, that whereas the traditional, transcendent theologies of the past two millennia have been decidedly hostile to the comic outlook, these new theologies, the theologies that have only emerged in the past two to three decades, are in a position to be remarkably hospitable to the comic spirit. It is not coincidental that comedy is slowly being admitted into theological thinking. The nature of the new immanent theologies virtually invites comedy in. Such theologies and the comic spirit are, in a real sense, cut from the same cloth. They like each other. They have emerged in the same era. They are intellectual and even ideological cousins, if not some closer relation. Since these new theologies are exerting an increasing influence on the thinking of preachers, particularly preachers who try to keep up on theological thinking and trends, it is not surprising at all that these same preachers should be inviting the comedic spirit into the pulpit with them as well. There is something of a revolution taking place around us. It is not just a revolution of comedy or of bringing comedy into the pulpit. It is a theological revolution, one whose comrade and confidant is the comic spirit itself.

3

The Nature of the Comic Sermon

What is a comic sermon? Is it just a funny sermon, one that makes people laugh? Or is there more to it than that? Yes, there is more to it than that; but one must begin by saying that the comic sermon not only welcomes laughter but often finds the preacher hoping to prompt laughter with the comic sermon, laughter of the kind that Hyers calls holy. The prompting of laughter, though, whether intentional or not, is *not* what distinguishes what we will call the comic sermon. In fact, it is possible to create and preach a comic sermon that induces no overt laughter from those who share it. One does not define a comic sermon in terms of its laugh quotient.

Instead, as was suggested in the previous chapter, the comic sermon must be understood much more in terms of the theological perspective that undergirds and motivates it. A comic sermon is one that finds its locus, at least in part, in what others have referred to as the human comedy; or, with a slight modification of Dante, it is a sermon based in the divine comedy, but starring human beings. This is a way of expressing two related theological ideas: one, that God, or the activity of the divine, is actively and fully present in the struggles, for better or worse, of human beings—whoever they are or wherever they are; and, two, that

the never-ending wrestling that human beings do, both person-
ally and collectively, to rise above themselves is divine activity—
however and wherever it takes place. There is considerable
theology implied in these companion statements, the kind of emergent theology that we discussed in the previous chapter. It is not
anthropology substituted for theology, but it is theology embodied in anthropology; it is theology "made flesh," not at some point
in the biblical past, but in the ongoing present and future of fal-
lible, foible-laden, confused, even crazy human activity.

When preaching takes place within this human context and
gives expression to this very human theological framework, the
comic sermon takes shape. The purpose of the sermon—the comic
sermon, then—is to nourish, explicate, encourage, and celebrate
both sides of that very human-divine, divine-human coin. The
sermon that embraces this dual struggle—of God in human form
and human searching as divine activity—becomes part of that
divine comedy with its fully human cast. The outcome is always
funny, often poignantly so, whether overt laughter is produced
or not—though it usually is.

The comic sermon, though, at least for the foreseeable future,
is not an either-or thing. It is a matter of degree during what most
likely will be a long transition from one theological paradigm to
another. Still, recognizing this will help many preachers come to
terms with the nature of the comic spirit as it appears in contemporary sermons, including their own. This means that a sermon,
on occasion, may be through and through a comic sermon, comic
in its theme, its development, in the pieces from which it is constructed. Such a thoroughly comic sermon will probably be fairly
rare, at least for most preachers. Fred Craddock's sermon in the
appendix of this book, "When the Roll Is Called Down Here,"
may come as close to that kind of thoroughgoing comic sermon
as one is likely to get today. Most of our sermons will be comic to
some degree by virtue of various amounts of comic "seasoning"
that we stir into them; and the range of comic elements that we
will explore in the next chapters of this book represent the kinds
of seasonings available to the preacher who wants to try the comic
sermon. Knowing this, though, lets one come into comic preaching gradually, a little here, a little there, more now, more later; at
the same time, it lets the preacher get a sense that the move to
comic preaching is, indeed, a profound one, based on a theological shift that needs to be acknowledged in the process of the move.

Having said all of this, though, we are still a long way from actually clarifying the nature of the comic sermon, particularly as it relates to preaching as it has been commonly understood. The comic sermon, in short, is surrounded by a series of misunderstandings that need to be addressed. When this is done, the comic sermon as a part of preaching comes more clearly and attractively into view. Here, then, we will discuss seven qualities that the comic sermon may be said to possess. Every comic sermon, in other words, should have these "marks" to some degree. Some may suggest that these should be the marks or qualities of every sermon, whether comic or not; and that would be true. But these are included here, not because they are unique to one kind of sermon as opposed to another, but because they are particularly important to what goes on in the making and preaching of a comic sermon.

Qualities of the Comic Sermon

First, the comic sermon must have a clear purpose and direction. This would seem to go without saying, since it is the first rule in every beginning homiletics textbook, but in talking about a comic sermon, it must not only be mentioned but also emphasized. Whether one likes the idea of a theme sentence, or proposition, or some other way of talking about a basic idea that motivates the sermon, every sermon—*including the comic sermon*—must have something to say. That nutshell "here-is-what-I-want-to say" idea may arise from a biblical text, from a particular problem in the lives of congregants, whether psychological or communal, or it may come as a doctrinal or theological matter, but such a guiding idea must undergird everything about the sermon. Whether the sermon is fashioned deductively or inductively, by a problem-solution or even a spiral paradigm, that idea must be present in some form. It is what homileticians have taught preachers for generations—and still do, by and large, as they should.

The reason for saying this is to emphasize that humor, comedy, or even laughter is *not* the purpose of the sermon. One does not preach to make people laugh. One does not engage in the comedic in any form in the pulpit for the sake of being comedic. What we are trying to grapple with, however, is that the sermon in our time seems to require a comedic flavor if it is not only to be heard but if it is to be understood, assimilated, and remembered. The issue that arises here concerns, at base, the entertainment value of the sermon. And the contention is that the renewal of today's sermon calls for the comedic, for some elements of humor, for some entertainment value, even though that is a notion that requires considerable care.

In a recent meeting of the Academy of Homiletics, the annual gathering of the men and women who teach preaching in seminaries, no less a homiletician than Henry Mitchell, the great African American scholar, presented a paper in which he discussed what he believes preaching is going to have to be to survive in the third millennium. He said that it is necessary to clarify the meaning of a couple of terms, one of which was entertainment. "We say that we don't believe in religion as entertainment," Mitchell said. "We believe in preaching *educational* sermons, not entertaining ones. Well, the opposite of entertaining is BORING, not educational. And unless we ENGAGE an audience, we need not try to teach them anything at all. Our problem is simply HOW to entertain with integrity, how to engage an audience compellingly, with the gospel, and for high purposes [his emphases]."[1] What Mitchell expressed is that it is time to quit putting down sermons that entertain, as though they are somehow not theological or even spiritual. It is time, instead, to embrace the idea that the pulpit is a place where something called entertainment not only can but *should* go on. Boredom fostered by the pulpit not only is not being tolerated by contemporary people, many of whom are now *former* churchgoers, but it will not be tolerated as a preaching paradigm of the future.

The comic sermon is designed, explicitly, to be entertaining or to have entertainment value. But it must, as Mitchell says, at the same time be *educational*. It must, at its root, have something to teach, something to say; and whatever that is, it must be clearly fixed in the preacher's heart and mind, and it must be the guiding thread for everything that is pulled into the sermon. The purpose and direction of the sermon, in other words, must be summed up in that educational and/or inspirational bedrock for what the preacher prepares. It is that very same sermon, though, that must be entertaining, that must be infused with a comic spirit. If it is not, as Mitchell says, it will tend to be educational, astute, and even spiritual, but, sadly, boring.

A Range of Emotions

The second mark of the comic sermon is that it encompasses a much wider range of emotions than does the non-comic sermon.

In short, it takes in not only the spectrum of what we might call the serious emotions, but also the complex comic emotions as well. These range from feelings of joyful anticipation and excitement to such diverse, if often subtle, feelings as glee, joviality, frivolity, jubilance, and mirth. Such emotional mixtures as surprise, buoyancy, even blissful acceptance are all part of the range of genuine comic feelings. These words are not synonyms, as some might think; they all express a different form and degree of comic response. They are the feelings that arise from the comic spirit, ones that the comic spirit, when embodied in a sermon, can conjure up. The comic sermon does not, of course, exclude the much better understood serious emotions (as we might call them), but it also seeks to incorporate the emotions that dominate the comic side of the coin. In that sense, the comic sermon reflects more of an emotional balance, we might say, a balance not of the mid-emotional range, but one that allows the emotional expressions of one side of the line to be balanced by the emotional expressions of the other.

To get a sense of this, one need only think about an episode of a classic situation comedy like *M*A*S*H*, which like few others managed also to play the full range of both serious and comic emotions. The show itself was dead serious. It was about life-and-death issues; it took personal relationships and showed their larger dimensions, sometimes as ethnic relationships, sometimes as gender relationships, sometimes as class or rank relationships, sometimes as political or even vocational relationships. The situations that were created were often profoundly comic, so the show was rightly considered a comedy. Yet along with the comedy and the comic emotions associated with laughter were always the serious emotions—the emotions of love and hate, of fear and dread, or of pain and sadness. One moment, the situation conjured up intense laughter, while in the next the tears could not be held back. We would laugh at Hawkeye or Frank and Hot Lips, or Winchester, at their comic pretensions, phoniness, and even goofiness; but then something would happen, just as in real life, that would break our hearts. A major part of the satisfaction that the show generated, and still does in reruns, was that it created an emotional experience of enormous range.

That is the intent of comic sermons as well. They are serious, dead serious, as they should be. There is no intention here to minimize the seriousness of life or the heart-wrenching situations that people, whether next door or around the world, find themselves in. Those situations, moreover, will, in a wide variety of ways, be a part of our sermons, as they should be. In that sense, our sermons must always be intensely serious. But when those dimensions of preaching are combined with the comic sensibility, the sermon creates a wide but balanced emotional range that results in the same type of human awareness and aesthetic satisfaction that many episodes of *M*A*S*H* achieved. To create sermons that reflect and conjure up that full range of emotions, from the serious through the comic, and to set those emotions in a gentle juxtaposition, is to create sermons that not only will attract people, but will engage people in the way that Henry Mitchell had in mind, sermons that, in that very engagement, will be profoundly entertaining.

This-Worldly Preaching

Third, the comic sermon is a this-worldly sermon. This is not surprising, since we have discussed both the immanence of the theology that undergirds it, and the human-divine, divine-human comedy on which it focuses. It is a sermon that wants to know who we are and how we got to be the way we are—with the "we" understood in a hundred different ways. It is a sermon that wants to know who our God is, who our gods are, and how such multiple gods (Gods) get along in our lives. It wants to know who in the world we *think* we are, we Christians as well as "we" non-Christians, and why we think what we do about ourselves. It wants to know about our silly senses of superiority, as well as our haunting inferiorities. It wants to know who we like and who we do not like, who we love and who we do not love, and why we find ourselves drawn to certain kinds of people and repelled by others.

The comic sermon wants very much to know about the secret, hidden places of our lives, and it sets out to dig up those places and talk aloud about them.[2] It wants to know about the relationship between those hidden places and our public ways of thinking and doing and being. The comic sermon would like for our secret and our public faces to interact, to match, to actually overlap and support each other. The comic sermon would like to know about the relationships between our beliefs and our behaviors, about the interplay of our innermost thinking about each other and how we actually treat each other. It would like to know about whether our public praying is in any way affected by our private praying and vice versa.

This can be seen in another way as well. The comic sermon is very much interested in theology and in the preaching of theology. Specifically, it wants to know not only what our theology is as we articulate it but, more importantly, it wants to know what our theology *actually* is, as we live it out day upon day. The comic sermon is profoundly concerned with our theological assumptions and the relationship between those assumptions and their human implications, whatever they are. It is also deeply interested in our theological pretensions and how they play themselves out in our processes of living, interacting, and even worshiping. The comic sermon is particularly interested, in other words, in how we square things among our theologies, our ideals, and our ethics, or how we live. It wants to infer, in fact, about our theologies by scrutinizing our ethics, a dangerous and often hilarious thing to do. The comic sermon, in this sense, is a nosy sermon, an audacious sermon. That, in fact, is why it is often a funny sermon. It wants to know about our private thoughts and actions as well as about our public pronouncements; in fact, it wants to know about them in tandem. It wants to know about their incongruities. It wants to know if we actually eat the mush that we sell on the street or in our pulpits and churches. It wants to know if we really believe the miracles that we go public with. It wants to know what our lives are like after dark, and whether those lives, in any way, resemble or do not resemble the lives that we live in the daylight.

Ironically, it should be understood that no one actually answers the questions that arise from these concerns; or, rather, one can only answer them for oneself and not for others. But the comic element does not lie in being able to answer the questions—as one can tell by listening to any good comedian; the comic element, rather, lies in the raising of the questions themselves. The comic element is in the wondering out loud. In fact, it is necessary for the preacher to be very cautious at this point, even though this wondering aloud is profoundly important to the comic sermon. The issues of this-worldly living and interacting that we raise are tough issues, so tough, in fact, that raising them in a comic spirit may be the *only* way of calling attention to them.

Most important, the preacher—no matter who the preacher is or how much the preacher calls on the Bible—has *no* answers to these issues. People must answer such matters for themselves. The preacher's task in the comic sermon is to set up the questions, set up the parameters for what amounts to comic thinking. These are "what if" matters and issues. What if—this? What if—that? What would we think—if? And so on. But they are real questions, real issues. The comic—and the comic sermon—calls us, we might say, to face things, to face ourselves, to face our inconsistencies, our incongruities, our illusions, and our deceptions. Who is to say that God is not in a sermon that does this? We are called on to be honest with ourselves, with each other—and with God. That is what a this-worldly comic sermon is like.

A Biblical Sermon

Fourth, and related to this, although perhaps surprising to some, the comic sermon is a biblical sermon; or at least it is to those of us who take the comic sermon seriously. The notion of what a biblical sermon is remains open to debate, of course, since any sermon that happens to make use of biblical material can be called a biblical sermon. But the comic sermon is biblical in the sense that it takes the Bible as an authentically human book, that is, as a collection of materials that profoundly reflect the human-divine, divine-human comedy actually being played out. Significantly, the Bible has relatively little piety as such in it. The stories of the First Testament, the Hebrew Scriptures in Christian form, are stunningly human stories—stories of intrigue and murder, of lust and incest, of power and greed, of corrupt kings and noble shepherds; the list goes on and on. On every page, the human-divine drama plays itself out in all of its comic glory. Myths are made to account for the unaccountable; the gods—or the God?—are appeased in a hundred ways; when one way fails, another is tried. There are the documents of wisdom, common meanderings of comic thought; there are the rantings of mad prophets; there are the dreamers who constantly conjure up silver linings.

In the New Testament, the stories are more focused, and we have already taken account of the comedy inherent in fragment after fragment of the gospel writings. Harvey Cox (among others) is correct: The whole Christ-myth is a comic play. The king wears thorns; the untaught fishermen wax eloquent; the persecutor becomes the persecuted one; those that Rome slaughters wear golden crowns around the celestial throne. The comic vision and comic spirit infuse the biblical texts at every point. To preach in a comic way is to draw on those comic elements—not just the narratives or the plots of the biblical writings, but on those very spirits today that the biblical writings set in motion in those first centuries of the new era.

Does the comic sermon actually draw on a biblical text? In most cases, the answer is yes; and in a later chapter we shall deal with some ways in which the comic spirit can approach the text in sermon preparation. What is important at this point, however, is that the comic spirit, while treating the text in a sacred way, does not, shall we say, bow before the text, any more than the court jester may be said to bow before the king that the jester serves. It engages the text in a comic fashion, clowning with it, playing with it, turning it on its head, sneaking up behind it, and so on. It wants to have fun with the text; and, in turn, it wants the text itself to have fun in the service of the sermon. So while it may all happen in ways that are unusual, even unexpected, as far as exegesis and sermon-making are concerned, the comic sermon has to be considered—or at least it considers itself—a biblical sermon.

Unfailing Hope

The fifth characteristic of the comic sermon, again closely related to the previous one, is that it always speaks unfailingly of hope and hopefulness. If it does not speak of it directly, as it sometimes is reluctant to do, it always implies a sense of "upness." Comic sermons are never downers. This is not because they are, by nature, funny, since for many such sermons funny is not an accurate description. They are comic sermons, in this sense, *because* they are not downers. They are not even happy, as such. The truth is that sometimes comedic elements can be downright painful, as we have seen, since a comic's honesty plows up deeply buried elements of life; still, the humor is in the confrontation with those elements. This can backfire, of course, and sometimes does; and both the comic and the preacher must stay constantly alert to such possibilities. But it is still the material of the comic vision, and confronting what are sometimes very difficult awarenesses often requires the ability to laugh.

What is important about the comic vision when it is brought to the comic sermon, though, is that it *assumes*—as was noted in the previous chapter—that what *is* is not what has to be. It assumes that our pretensions can be stripped away. It assumes that when we become aware of the discrepancies and incongruities of our lives, we at least have a shot as at fixing them, at giving our lives a wholeness and honesty that we take as the central call of righteous living. It assumes that, if we listen carefully to ourselves, we can, like Garrison Keillor's Hopeful Gospel Quartet, sing better tomorrow the song that we sang just so-so today. The comic vision assumes that when we wear no clothes and someone has the courage and the audacity to tell us about it, we will want to go get dressed. It assumes that when we are exhibiting a mean spirit, cloaked as a form of kindness, and a jester makes us laugh by ironically calling attention to our meanness, we might want to shed that meanness and become truly kind. That may not always be true, of course. Sometimes we will only laugh at our meanness and at our jester, and go on being mean, set to laugh at it again some other time.

That is not the view, though, that motivates the comic and the comic spirit. The comic spirit believes otherwise. In fact, the comic spirit believes that if we laugh at our meanness this time, and go on being mean, there will surely be another time; and the next time, perhaps, the meanness will be laughed at in a way that will bring some sober self-recognition and perhaps, just perhaps, that will be the time for ending the meanness. The hope of the comic spirit springs virtually eternal.

More than this, the comic spirit is not inclined to summon, shall we say, the "gods" to fix things and bring hope into a hope-short situation. In that sense, the comic outlook also stands somewhat at odds with much traditional religion, including traditional or orthodox Christianity. Since the comic spirit is an immanent spirit, and comic theology is an immanent theology, change arises, it believes, from divine machinations at work deep within the human heart and community. Hope arises, that is, because of the belief that humans can change, and that various forms of awareness, consciousness, and human pressures can and do, in fact, effect change. This is not to say that God, however the Christian God is conceived, does not have a role to play in the twists and turns of human history and change; it is to say, though, that the workings of God arise from the human psyche and collective, aided often by the role of comic jesters, whether they be secular or sacred. When we laugh at ourselves and our human connections to others, we are, from the comic perspective, freed to look at ourselves and how we encounter ourselves and others. When we laugh at our silly ways, at our stupidities and crudities, we are freed, as it were, to acknowledge them. That gives us the hopeful option of changing what, and even who, we are. It sounds like a reach, and no doubt it is, but it is still the idea that motivates the comic spirit. Ironically, it is also the idea that motivates the Christian gospel.

Connecting and Playing

The sixth characteristic of the comic sermon goes beyond an engagement with those who share our preaching, even beyond entertaining, as important as both of those things are. The comic sermon actually provides a remarkable way of *connecting* with the congregants and, more importantly perhaps, connecting them with each other. The bond that comedy, or the sharing of laughter, makes possible is unlike any other bond that can tie human beings together. It is a *forging* of people that begins in a shared symbolic experience—that is we like the same thing so we really like each other—but that surrounds that shared experience with a warmth that not only bonds but even congeals the connections that are made. It is the power not just of sharing, but of sharing laughter which adds an additional cement to every common experience. It is the sharing of laughter that turns a wonderful experience of togetherness into a veritable celebration, one to be repeated again and again, literally as a natural part of one's life.

It is at this point that we become most conscious of the relationship between comedy and laughter and the notion of play or playing. Many scholars have called attention to the fact that to play is to laugh, even though much play is done, as we might say, in dead earnest. This sermon, in this sense, can be seen as a form of the preacher and congregants "playing together." The solidarity can be that intense when the comic processes of play are invoked. To create a comedic sermon is to conjure up for all involved what Johan Huizinga called "sacred performance," performance, that is, filled with nothing short of deep anticipation and sacred interweaving. Such a sacred performance, Huizinga wrote in his classic study, *Homo Ludens* (*Humans at Play*), is "more than a symbolical actualization—it is a mystical one. In it, something invisible and inactual takes beautiful, actual, holy form." The participants become convinced that they are living in a time and place, in an order of things, higher than that in which they actually live. The space in which they play is sacred space; it is marked out; there are boundaries that must not, during the playing, be violated. But when the playing is over, the effect is not lost, either. It "continues to shed its radiance on the ordinary world outside," a radiance that gives security, order, and even a kind of prosperity to the whole community until the time for playing comes around again.[3]

Such is a remarkable description, if not for what the sermon actually is, at least for what we would like it to be. It is the sermon as comic event, as *play-event*, where laughter, celebration, and fun are all rolled into one. It is also instructive at this level to think about the relation between the comic sermon and the sermon in its more liturgical, or ritualistic, forms. In some free-church Christian traditions, the sermon is viewed as a kind of stand-alone event, often, in fact, standing at the center of the worship experience itself. Here there is relatively little difficulty in coming to terms with the sermon as a comic event or process, an event where laughter can and should take place. In other Christian traditions, however, the sermon is viewed as much more a liturgical event, meaning that the sermon is melded within the overall liturgical experience, usually imbued with all of the solemnity and formality of the liturgy itself.

What Huizinga reminds us of, however, is that the religious rituals of ancient cultures, no matter how solemn, retained a strong "play" element, an element, even in the solemnity, of fun and celebration, if not spontaneous laughter. Play and religious ritual, he says, have existed as part of each other for as far back as we are able to chart human experience. Throughout human history, "the concept of play merges quite naturally with that of holiness." In Huizinga's words:

> Primitive, or let us say, archaic ritual is thus sacred play, indispensable for the well-being of the community, fecund of cosmic insight and social development but always play in the sense Plato gave to it—an action accomplishing itself outside and above the necessities and seriousness of every life. In this sphere of sacred play the child and the poet are at home with the savage.[4]

In short, the comic vision and spirit, based as it is in the spirit of play, is not reserved only for what is sometimes called the free-church sermon. It is also, if we let it be, a part as well of the sermon within the liturgical church's more ritualistic settings. The liturgical ritual as play can be effectively joined by the sermon as play. The sermon's comic spirit and flavor can be merged with the playfulness, indeed the comic spirit,of the ritualized processes of worship. It is not too much to suggest that if the sermon should come to be viewed as a comic creation, with all that that suggests of playfulness, it could go a long way toward spreading its comic spirit over the rest of the liturgical features that congregants share in worship. The goal of it all is human solidarity, human connectedness. The liturgy makes its contribution to that, and at no time better than when that liturgy has the spontaneous, serious feel of play. When the comic sermon, with its own form of playfulness and mirth, is added to that, the result can be electrifying.

An Original Sermon

Finally, there is one other characteristic of the comic sermon that flows from those that we have already noted. It is that the comic sermon is an *original* sermon. That, too, is a strange assertion to make, since it is assumed that every sermon is an original one. But this means something quite different from that. In the orthodox (or neo-orthodox) sense, for preaching to be biblical preaching, its message had to originate from the Bible, from a particular biblical text, and that message had to be formulated and spoken without the interference or even intrusion of the preacher. In fact, the assumption was that the way to nullify a sermon's power or effectiveness was to let the preacher's own experience cloud the clarity of the biblical "witness." The comic spirit in preaching, though, not only disagrees with that viewpoint, but asserts that a sermon's power—at least in the contemporary world—is directly commensurate with the degree to which it is explicitly *informed* by the preacher's own experience.

From the comic viewpoint, this means two basic things, as far as a sermon's originality is concerned—things that we shall build upon in numerous ways in the pages that follow. The first is the requirement that one who would preach a comic sermon must learn to think about, and speak about, old things in new ways. The comic vision requires freshness. It requires an original spirit. It requires that what is said in the sermon not be "canned," that it not come straight from the commentary, though new directions can sometimes start there; it requires that what is said not come from any kind of packaged sources, particularly when those packages are available to others, whether past or present. The comic sermon takes risks in originality, as we shall see later. In the secular world, no great comic would ever have been successful without taking enormous risks with both outlook and material. Not everything works or works ideally, to be sure, but the risks of originality are crucial to making the comic sermon sparkle. And they are essential to the comic sermon's creation of new biblical and human insight. By and large, audiences—congregations—appreciate risk-taking, something that is often quite recognizable; and when that risk-taking is done in a spirit of joy, laughter, and playfulness, the ability of the soul to comprehend and embrace new things is simply remarkable.

There is a second dimension to the idea of originality in the comic sermon, though. It has to do with the need for the sermon to reflect the preacher's own living of real life in the real world. The comic sermon is not an ivory-tower sermon; indeed, it simply cannot be. It assumes that the preacher knows himself or herself, and, more importantly, that the preacher knows *people*. One wants to say that the comic sermon, in its originality, must reflect the preacher's own experience of the world; but saying it that way is misleading, as we shall see in more detail in the next chapter. The comic sermon acknowledges, though, that the preacher is a real person, living, working, shopping, playing, driving kids to school, going to soccer games, struggling to make ends meet, feeling angry at times on the freeway, and on and on and on. No two people are alike, however; so one can surmise that no two preachers are ever alike either—not only theologically or homiletically, but (more importantly?) as real people. The preacher's week is full, like anyone else who hustles to make a living. It is full of work, of course, but it is also full of many other things, things that crowd in and that are often crowded out because there is simply not enough time. In all of that—even granted that the full week of work is church-related—the preacher struggles with faith, with his or her own faith; and that struggle with faith is no easier for the preacher than for any of the laypeople who make the church, its worship and its programs, a part of their lives. In short, here, the sermon's originality must somehow reflect one person's—the preacher's—own unique struggle with faith. The preacher cannot speak for all the faith of all time, as though one had some large seat in the sky; and using the Bible does not give one that omniscient perspective, either. The preacher lives in a real-world context, and sees even the Bible through that context; and, to be original and authentic, the sermon must not only reflect but also embrace that limitation. Ironically, it is that very limitation that opens the door to the comic spirit in the pulpit.

Still, two things must be faced here, and faced squarely, since both of these things tend to neutralize the strength of that contextual perspective of the preacher. First, the preacher must constantly be on guard against assuming a privileged position for his or her own real-world living. As we shall see in the next chapter, the preacher tells his or her own stories, but they are not to be stories "about" the preacher—they are to be the stories of others, as those others are encountered by the preacher in the living of real life. The difference will be fundamental. The second thing that must be firmly grasped is that the preacher's experience of living and life is never, by virtue of its contextualization, universal; nor can it be. This means that the preacher, while being fully cognizant of the comic resources that arise from his or her own circumstances and situations, must be equally aware that countless people live in circumstances and situations that are totally different from those of the preacher. The preacher cannot change this, of course; but what the preacher *can* do, beyond maintaining keen awareness of it, is to become an unrelenting student of the lives and circumstances of those who live in continguous but fundamentally different worlds. The comic vision brought to the sermon not only knows oneself, but is profoundly empathetic and compassionate toward the real lives of other people. There are overlaps, even within fundamental difference; and one will come to appreciate and embrace those overlaps. But the comic vision knows difference when it sees it; and it works to take full account of that difference, even in the framing of real stories of real people, whoever they are.

There are no doubt other aspects to what we are calling the comic sermon. And even these will exist only in degrees in the various sermons that one prepares and preaches. After having said all this, though, can we actually define a comic sermon? Probably not. Perhaps the best we can do is note, at this stage at least, that the comic sermon is not a "free-for-all." It is not, by any means, an "anything goes" conglomeration in the pulpit. It has something to say, something specific, concrete, and serious. But behind that is a particular, highly original outlook, one composed of theological, biblical, spiritual, anthropological, and creative strands. What should also be clear at this stage is that the comic sermon is not a certain kind of "performance" from the pulpit, not something wild or ragtag. And while in a later chapter we shall discuss the specific problems of preaching a comic sermon, such a sermon is not primarily about how one preaches. The comic sermon is a particular kind of sermon, meticulously prepared and crafted. It is, as we have said, a playful sermon, but it is, at the outset and above all, the playfulness of preparation before it is the playfulness of presentation.

Part II

The Ingredients of the Comic Sermon

4

The Comic Story: Foundation of the Comic Sermon

Stories and storytelling, not jokes, form the bedrock of the comic spirit. This includes stories that are shared by anyone at any time in any place, from simple stories told informally around a dinner table to stories that are elaborately written into novels, plays, or movies. It includes stories that are conjured from memory or imagination to those that are meticulously researched and fashioned. Whatever they are, stories are the prototype of all human comedy. They are also the basic ingredient of the comic sermon.

There are two reasons why the story is the bedrock of the comic sermon. The first is because, in a sense, all human stories are comic stories, since human storytelling itself is a comic art. The key word here is human. There are tragic stories, of course, but, as we have already suggested, they tend to be stories of humans and their gods or their fates, or stories of the cosmic, beyond-human-control circumstances of their lives. There can be comic stories of God or the gods, of course, but only if the cosmic is interpreted through or planted firmly in the world of the human. Those stories that we will call human stories, even human stories of life, death, tears, and grief, are stories that mix tears with laughter. As Hugh Duncan has pointed out, the comic sensibility is synonymous with the ups and downs of human struggle, with the persistence of hope in the human spirit. When human interaction and activity is at the center of the storytelling, whatever the story's motivation or emotional outcome, the result is invariably a comic story.

The second reason why the story is the basic ingredient of the comic sermon is because the story most readily serves as the carrier of the numerous other comic forms that light up human discourse. Humor is created in many ways, and in the next few chapters we will discuss the most basic ones—surprise, juxtaposition, incongruency, the twists and turns of metaphor and language—but in preaching these will not tend to exist in isolation. Of course they can, and sometimes do, but their comic weight or effect is usually very thin. It is the story form that most effectively calls into play the various comic tools. Hence the foundational nature of the comic story in the sermon.

At its core, a story has two defining characteristics. The first is well-defined movement, progression; that is, a story must have a beginning, a middle, and an ending, and it must move, however swiftly, through these stages. The second characteristic is that the story must incorporate detail, color, and texture. It must, in short, come to life. One must be able, in sharing the story, to visualize what is happening, must be able to sense the story's place and time, its "feel," and must be able to get caught up in the action or the movement as the story is told. The better these graphic aspects are developed in the story—using setting, description, and dialogue—the more involving and memorable the story becomes.

Some will point out that these kinds of things have always been in the sermon, but in the past they have been called "illustration" rather than "story." If one looks closely at the illustrations of master preachers of the past, however, one becomes aware that illustrations are *not* stories in the way that we have described or defined the story. Instead, illustrations are what might be called "fragments of narrative information," well-chosen pieces of information or experience, short on movement or progression as well as short on texture and color that only details can provide. Let me give an example of an excellent, and typical, illustration from a sermon by James Cox, a master of illustration. It is from a sermon titled "Foolish Fatalism," which appeared in his book, *Surprised by God*:

In 1963 I made my first trip to New York City. I arrived by taxi at Hastings Hall of the Union Theological Seminary, where I was to stay during a few weeks of study, and deposited my bags. Then I went outside and walked past the Riverside Church and across the street, where I stood and looked for a while at the interesting sights across the Hudson River. As I walked back to my room, I looked across the street at the Jewish Theological Seminary and saw something that struck me more forcefully than the Riverside Church or the view across the Hudson River. On the front of the building was a sculpture of the burning bush with an inscription: "The bush burned but it was not consumed." I was struck by that sculpture and that inscription because in them was wrapped up the key to the courage and survival of the Jewish people. The presence and power of God in all of the holocausts of history enabled them to endure. God had promised; they believed God's promise, and that was that![1]

There is, I know, a bit of movement in this paragraph, from Professor Cox's trip to New York City to the walk he took. It lets him set up the inscription which he came onto: "The bush burned but was not consumed"; it is the line that embodies the point he wishes to make. This is not, however, a story, but only a fragment of one. While it has a beginning, which could become a story, it has no development and certainly no ending. The point that Professor Cox elaborates, based on the inscription, is not an ending or the conclusion to the story. A story also requires what we have called color and texture, which is enough detail so that one can empathetically participate in what is going on. Professor Cox does not set out to provide that—he wants to move as quickly as possible to the inscription from which his point was made.

Stories Are Well Developed

One should now turn to the sermon in the Appendix by Professor Craddock, "When the Roll is Called Down Here." It has in it both illustrations *and* stories. The sermon is *opened* and *closed* with a story—the story of the jury roll call at the beginning and the story of the baptism at Watts Bar Lake at the end. In between are some story "fragments," much like Professor Cox's illustrations—Craddock's illustration of the quilt and the one of the visit to the Vietnam Wall. The stories in the sermon, however, are different. They are not just longer; they are well developed. In both cases, one finds not only a beginning and then progression or development, but also a "closing" with each story—not commentary about the story, but a place to which the story itself leads. In the first story, the jury summons is described in striking detail, which is the story's opening. It then turns to the roll call itself, its development, tracking through various elements in the jury "list." It ends with the woman sitting next to Craddock—the German woman who heard something quite unexpected in the "list." The story also has remarkable detail, and because of the detail—the sense of place, the dialogue, the ambiance of situation—one has a sense of "being there" for the roll call.

In the sermon's concluding story of Watts Bar Lake, again a carefully detailed opening is present—the baptism service is set up. We are then taken through the ritual of the service as the people gather around the fire, which represents the progression of the story. Then it has an ending, which is the explanation that Percy Miller provides to the young preacher. Both stories, moreover, are serious pieces, filled with human comedy at the same time. Both break open the pain and the joy of living, of being with other people, of participation in human struggle and hope. This is the stuff of humor, of the comic spirit.

But what are such stories for? What purpose do they serve in the sermon? It becomes clear when one looks closely that such stories are not for the purpose of "illustration," at least not in the way in which that term has been used in the past. Stories serve at least three functions in a sermon, with some stories serving one, others two, and some all three functions at the same time. The first is that stories often play a *parabolic* role in the sermon. They speak as a parable speaks. They have meaning or a point, but the meaning or point is actually *embodied* in the story itself. The story can be commented on, and sometimes that may be a useful thing, but often those who share the parabolic story are simply left to find their own meaning or meanings in it. The same may be said, of course, of Jesus' parables. Good stories may be thought of as the equivalent of Jesus' parables, since most of the parables attributed to him are, at the very least, decent stories. Even in Jesus' parables, meanings are often ambivalent, as those who preach them know only too well. Or the meanings of the parables that we try to articulate seem superfluous, since any thinking person can extract from the story some insight that connects to the living of one's own life.

A second role that stories, comic stories, play in the sermon is the creation of *shared experience*. It is true that we concluded the previous chapter with observations about the preacher's own experiences, and here we are concerned about the preacher's own stories. We noted that the preacher must be very careful not to take his or her own life and life stories as either privileged or universal. The preacher's stories are not unique and should not come across as unique, because they are the *preacher's* stories; the preacher's stories are not universal, either, which means that the preacher must constantly be attuned to those who are *omitted* from the telling of his or her stories. Having said that, however, the process of human storytelling is probably the most universal, and universally understood, activity that human beings of all kinds can engage in with each other. There are common human experiences that, if one looks for them and treats them sensitively, cross many human boundaries. In fact, this may be one of those things that sets storytelling apart from virtually every other form of human discourse.

Stories can take our deepest experiences and connect them to the experiences of other people—sometimes in contrasting ways, but most often in cooperative and coordinated ways. We share our feelings with each other in the sharing of our stories. When those stories are shared from the pulpit, they become the stories that draw people closer together. When the preacher tells a story drawn from the wedding of his or her daughter, weaving it into the fabric of the sermon, that story is not an egotistical expression of the preacher but is, instead, a means of conjuring up wedding stories throughout most of the congregation. And while that story may not call up other wedding stories per se, since everyone may not have a "wedding story," it often, for others, can conjure up stories similar in substance to the wedding story. Preacher, your wedding story reminded me of the time when my wife... Every good story will do that. Lives are connected. Experiences of one become bridges to the experiences of others. One person's probing story becomes a welcomed invitation to the problem of similar experiences in the lives of those who share the pulpit's story. Every preacher who has used stories within the sermon knows that connecting power, a power that can often become almost quite visible, as a story is unfolded. The good storyteller also learns that, even in telling a story about, say, a wedding, one can take account of those who have no similar story of their own—and in that taking account add that sensitively told story to the experience of others who, in turn, can relate to it. It is very complex, of course; but the creativity of it all, at its base, is community-building. It is not coincidental that the gospel accounts are constructed overwhelmingly of storytelling.

A third role that the story often plays in the sermon is a behavioral role; the story, that is, can have a "go thou and do likewise" effect. Stories, in fact, provide the clearest form of teaching behavior, since they work not in didactic terms but in the form of an invitation. They provide what Kenneth Burke has called at one point "equipment for living" and at another "strategies for situations." The story sets up a situation and shows how someone, or several people, acted in that particular situation; and then the story tells, or at least suggests, the outcome of the particular action taken in that situation. Burke contends that stories are crucial to human community because they form the catalogue of acceptable behaviors for living within the "situations" of that particular community. This applies whether the stories come through nursery rhymes, the fables of childhood, the novels of adult life, the soap operas of afternoon television, or the sitcoms of an evening in front of the set. We learn how people act or have acted in specific situations, and we are able to shape our own actions in similar situations based on our "definitions" of those actions.

This "go thou and do likewise" dimension of storytelling is seldom done in a direct way. It is, instead, usually done by analogy: The situation I find myself in is *somewhat* like a situation I remember from a story; or it reminds me of a situation I once read about, and the character got out of it by... I can't do that right now, but if I act this way, it will be "like" what that character did that made things come out right. It is that kind of analogical thinking that the story sets up; and, in fact, the story may set up a bank of memories that will only come into play in an analogical fashion much later in one's life.

A major part of the power of story, though, is that the story belongs to the teller. The preacher, in short, should tell her or his own stories in order for the power of storytelling, and comic storytelling in particular, to work. Thus, it is not coincidental that the key stories of Prof. Craddock's sermon are his stories, stories from his past, one recent, the other long past. The comic spirit and the comic sermon nudge us to tell our own stories, not the stories that we have picked up from some other place or even the stories of literature that we have read, as important as those can sometimes be. It is the preacher's own stories, though, that become truly comic and memorable in the telling, stories that arise from the life and experience, the looking and listening, of one sensitive storyteller.

The Problem of Egotism

There is a problem here, though, one that must be dealt with very carefully. It is the problem that many preachers and homileticians who are wary of stories, particularly one's own stories, are quick—and justified—in raising. It is the problem of egotism that seems to underlie that act of the preacher telling his or her own stories from the pulpit. It is the idea that telling one's own stories gives a sense of "look at me" or "this is how I did it," a sense clearly unfit for the humility of the pulpit. What we are starting to realize, however, is that it is possible for one to capture the full power of telling one's own stories in the pulpit while at the same time avoiding the serious pitfall of egotism, or egoism.

Three rules must be followed if the preacher is to tell personal stories without conveying an egotistic impression. The first is that the story that is told must be about others, and not "about" the preacher. This is how the preacher is able to take full account of his or her own contextual life-experience, while—at the same time—not assuming some unique or privileged role in the stories that are shared from the preacher's life. This also is what requires the preacher to become a relentless observer and recorder of the lives and experiences of other people, real people, usually unknown people, as far as the preacher is concerned. The preacher may be, and usually is, a character in the story that is told, sometimes an observer on the sidelines, identified as such, sometimes an actual participant in the story. This, in fact, is what gives the story its personal power, its flavor that enables one to be "in the story" with the teller. But the spotlight of the story is to fall on someone else, someone tangential to the preacher. The preacher is the set-up person, the narrator, the "stage manager" of Wilder's *Our Town*, visible, always present, who keeps the story intimate and tense, but always unobtrusively. The second rule is related to this: The storyteller, the preacher, is never to be the "hero" of the story or its "villain." Those are spotlight roles, and they must always be reserved for someone else. The proper role for the preacher as storyteller, if a role is played, is that of the learner, the one who profits from what goes on in the situation and event of the story. The third rule, too, is tied to the first two. The preacher or storyteller should not become either preachy or moralistic about the story or its development. Stories may have asides, but seldom commentary. This does not mean that stories may not have clearly stated morals or points—but they should come from the mouth of a key character in the story being told and not as something added by the preacher or the storyteller.

When one looks back on the stories at the beginning and at the end of Craddock's sermon, one finds these rules followed meticulously—which is why one does not hear (or read) the sermon with any sense that the preacher is surely engaged in a egotistical thing here, telling his own stories like that. Such an idea never crosses one's mind in the engagement with the sermon. The first story has the teller, the preacher, as a narrator, setting up a situation, and then the preacher settles in, as he says, to "take notes." At that point the story is about all of those names, those people on the jury "list." And with the storyteller, we get caught up in the names as he describes them. Then gradually the story's focus shifts to the woman next to him. He listens to her; he chats, of course—the storyteller is there, a visible participant in the story, but the story ends up being about her, about what she went through, what she remembers. It is, in a nutshell, her story that we are told, which is why we never think that the preacher is being egotistical in telling us her story. If the story has a hero, she is it; the storyteller, fascinated, stands outside the spotlight. Moralizing? If there is anything of it at all, it comes from her: She remembers, and in that roll call situation, it comes back to her. And the preacher, like those to whom the story is told, listens and learns from her.

The same dynamics are at work in the concluding story of the sermon. The young preacher is there, it is his story, but at no point is the story about him. It is the story of that church and its baptismal service. The preacher, as storyteller, is the narrator. He sets up the story; he describes the activity, including his role in the process. But the story is unmistakably about them. And it is about Percy Miller, who more or less directs the show. He is the one who signals its close, who stays behind to kick sand over the fire, who gives the young preacher the "sermon" about what church, after all, is about. The storyteller takes it all in, becomes the off-camera voice, even though he has been a character in this church's annual rite. There is no egotism whatsoever here from the preacher, the one who tells the story. It is his story—the preacher's story; no one else could even tell the story as he does—but it is not his story at all. It is the story of that Watts Bar Lake church, of Percy Walker and the baptismal service.

When the rules are followed, there is no egotism in the stories. Yet the power of the stories remains their intensely personal dimension, as far as the storyteller is concerned. That power in large part derives from the credibility of the preacher's own experience of the stories, the fact of the preacher's participation in what is told. In other words, neither of the two stories of Craddock's sermon would have the power that they have without the participatory role played by the storyteller in each. Without that, both stories would be adrift, nice in their telling, somewhat involving perhaps, but sanitized, sterilized. It is the storyteller's "being there," and then telling the story of being there, of watching and listening, of catching something "as it is happening," that adds the sparkle, the passion, and the intensity to both stories, and to all stories like these. If the storyteller was there—really there—and tells us the story, then we, too, are "really there," and the electricity is in that sense of actual involvement that can be achieved in no other way.

Finding Stories Everywhere

Where does one find stories for the comic sermon? The answer is: in the full range of one's own life and experience, not as some kind of a "special person" who lives in story-like fashion, but as a normal person whose life, like every life, is composed of vignette upon vignette, episode after episode. The trick is in learning to see and keep records of the story living and unfolding process. Some live through wonderful stories and never see them. Did anything happen to you today? No, not much really. Been kind of dull. Others more keenly tuned—and this is a process that one learns—find stories everywhere, and they are always there to be found. Let me tell you what happened while I was shopping today...

For years, I have done what I now urge my students to do and that is to keep a daily notebook. Mine has always been a stenographer's pad; and every evening, just before turning out the light, I reflect on the day and find one experience, something that happened, something I watched, some encounter with another person, something that took place at church or after church, or at school, or at the hospital, at the grocery store, or wherever. Something that could be a story. It could have been a particular experience that I was only tangentially involved in, one that I saw. It could have been something that someone did to me or for me—or for someone else, and I was nearby. It could have been a comment, something off-hand even, that someone said, that took me back to another time and place, to an experience from my long-distant past; and so I would call up from memory that experience and it would become my "story page" for that day. Sometimes it would be something large and important that provided not a single story, but a series of stories, short takes, each with an unfolded form of its own; and I would try to get each one down, a page for this one and another page for that one. I would write down no more than a single stenographer's page, a few paragraphs at most, capturing the story, not too long, and yet with enough background, dialogue, and detail so that even years later I could call it up and tell it again. Few things have served my preaching more effectively than my story notebook. A notebook like this would contain stories like the reading of the jury summons list and that woman who sat next to me, and a recollection from early ministry of Percy Walker and the Watts Bar Lake baptismal service. Pages from a kept book. What is necessary for the preacher is the discipline of story collecting, the conscious discipline of seeing or sensing the story, and then remembering it until it can be put down on paper.

All of the stories that one collects, of course, are not comic stories. In fact, my experience has been that one does not set out to "find" comic stories; nor does one say that one will only record the stories that are funny, the stories that are comic. In the collecting and meticulous note-taking, one does not make any such distinction. Many stories that one records, in fact, will be deeply serious, even painful; and yet they must be recorded, too. Stories only become comic stories in the telling, and in the next few chapters, we will consider various dimensions of that storytelling. As everyone knows, what is very serious, embarrassing, and even hurtful when it happens often becomes very funny in retrospect as our bumbling, inept ways reveal themselves at the root of those things that go haywire in our lives. Distance itself has a way of revealing the comedic in the midst of the pain.

Let me turn for a few moments to one of my story notebooks and pick at random from it. First, I will share a story, sketched in my notebook, one that I am able even now to reconstruct, though I wrote it down a long time ago:

It was late at night, about 10 o'clock, and as Snoopy would say, it was cold and rainy. I had been to a long meeting at school, a contentious meeting, and I was feeling, to say the least, out of sorts. Still, I had clear instructions from my wife to stop at the Kroger store on my way home and pick up a few things—cat food, always cat food, some corn flakes, milk, and bananas, as I remember. I didn't want to stop, but I knew that if I didn't—well, there would be some price to pay when I got home. So I pulled in at Kroger's, got out into the black rain, and went in. Not many people were there that late at night. I got a cart and began my hunt. I knew where the cat food was so I headed there first. I hunted for the Fancy Feast, but I couldn't find it. Finally, I decided on a substitute, threw a half dozen cans in my cart, and headed down the aisle looking for whatever was next on my list.

Just as I rounded the shelves at the end of the aisle, a woman came from the other direction, heading up my cat food aisle. As she passed, I heard her humming to herself. She never looked at me, but I recognized the tune. Hmm-hmm hmm hmmmm hmmmmm; hmm-hmm hmm hmmmmmm…It was Blessed Assurance, Jesus Is Mine…the old hymn. I hadn't heard it in quite a while and it caught me. I pushed on down the aisle, found the corn flakes, and headed for the milk. Without meaning to—in fact, without wanting to: I was feeling out of sorts—I must have picked up the song and was humming it to myself now—hmm hmm hmm hmmmm, hmmmm, hm hm hm hmmmmmm—but reluctantly, mind you. I did not notice the man coming up behind me with his cart, but as he pulled alongside me, he said, "Nice song," and he pushed in front of me. Now, he was humming, hmmm hmmm hmmm hmmmmmmmm, hmmmmmmmmm, blessed assurance, Jesus is mine. I swear we must have been the only people in the store. I stopped and caught myself. It was an old hymn, a strange hymn, I thought to myself; and I don't think I had sung it since I was very young. Now I was humming it again. My step picked up; my mood changed. I found the milk and the bananas and decided to hurry to the front of the store to say thank you to that woman who had been humming it first.

When I got to the cashier, the woman was gone, and so was the man who had picked up the song from me. There was only the young cashier with the blond hair pulled back into a ponytail.

"You seem happy for such a rainy night," she said as she grabbed the cans of cat food.

"Yes, I guess I am," I replied, "but…" and I stopped myself. "Yes, I am," was all that would come out.

I paid her, took my sack, and left. The dark night was not as dark as it was. The rain had let up.

It is a simple story, a true story, one that can be told in a straightforward manner. I have used it in a sermon on the contagion of good things, of good deeds, of the ways in which small things seem to be passed along in the most unexpected of ways. For me, it has served the purpose that all good stories should fill—it is parabolic, as we sketched that earlier; it conjures up some shared experience, since my experience of the grocery store will cause others to respond with a "yeah, that reminds me of the time when…"; and it is a "go thou and do likewise"—not as I did in the story, but as that first person did, the one who started the chain of events that evening at the grocery store.

Some will suggest that the story has a triteness about it, that it does not speak about the gospel, about the great facts of biblical theology, that it is just a little thing that happened, something that, in a sermon, would just get in the way of really trying to say something important. That is a view, however, that I simply do not accept, one that harks back to a view of theology that, in my judgment, is passing. If one believes, as I do, that the points of theological light are small and that they too often pass unnoticed while one watches for the big spotlights, then a story like this becomes a way to find and focus on the presence of God in the insignificant, as people, in a sense, pass that presence back and forth to each other. The theology that seems important to me is that which is hidden in the cracks and crevices of life, in things that take place late at night in very non-church places, and among people whose religions are often veiled. That is where comic theology tends to be located. It is what I take the theology of Jesus' parables to be. So in the trite stories one finds the gems, the glimmers, over which we pass so easily, which we often dismiss as not theologically substantive. In these stories, though, as simple and common as they seem, if one has eyes to see and ears to hear, one just might find some still, small voice at work.

But let me share some other stories from my notebook, ones that, for me, also have potential for a comic sermon at some point along the line:

> There is my evening of driving a borrowed white Rolls Royce automobile and being absolutely amazed and even shaken at the taunts and jeers of all kinds of people on the street and in other automobiles toward me and what I was driving. When I told the owner about such behavior, she said, sure, that just goes with driving such a car, and that she solves the problem by always driving with the windows up so that she cannot hear anything, and she never looks from side to side out of the window when she stops at a traffic light. My story notes include the circumstances of my being in the automobile, the set-up, as well as a description of the responses of people to me and the car. They conclude with my conversation with Kay, the owner, at the end of the evening. And even though I am the one who drove the car, I tell it as an agonizing story of Kay, the owner of that car, and the people that she encountered who saw that car as a symbol of something that they detested.
>
> There is my experience of standing in a grocery-story check-out line watching the people in front of me. A woman with two small children was struggling with her food stamps and still coming up two dollars short. She was on the verge of crying, when the man behind her, just in front of me, unobtrusively put two dollar bills under his finger and slid them forward along the conveyer belt toward her. He caught her eye and she took the bills, mouthing the words "thank you" to him. She smiled at him like I have never seen anyone smile

before. My notes provide a fairly complete description of the entire experience.

I sat in a bank one afternoon waiting to talk with an official. While I waited, an elderly man came in followed by two younger men, dressed, well, shabbily. They stood in a teller line, saying nothing. When it was their turn at the window, they went together. I overheard the old man trying to draw out his money, though he knew very little about how to do it. The teller picked up on that and began questioning him, while the two younger ones were getting nervous. The teller knew the old man, and it was soon clear that she was making conversation, trying to stall him, or them. The younger men became belligerent, but the teller talked with them, too, managing to keep them calm. Without the three of them even becoming aware of it, two policemen had entered through the back, walked up behind them, and took the two young fellows into custody. A bank official sat down and calmly soothed the old man.

Our 16-year-old cat died. What a beaut she was. At the end, she had contracted cancer and we had spent a good deal of money on her treatment. There are three stories in my notebook about Cowslip, that wonderful, luxurious cat. There is the story of the difficult day on which she died. The vet sent her home with us saying she only had a few hours but she wasn't in any pain. For hours we took turns petting her as she lay as comfortably as we could make her; through Saturday night, we petted her and watched over her. She died about 5 a.m. on Sunday morning, just as the sun was coming up. I wrote the story in my notebook that Sunday night. It is a sad, comic story about an animal that had been a constant companion to my wife for almost all of those sixteen years.

The second Cowslip story had to do with the extreme grief my wife felt over the loss of that pet. But there was no real crying that Sunday morning; everything happened as it was expected to happen and the pain was by and large kept in check. Church people of years past knew Cowslip—they had been at our house many times—and when they got word that Cowslip had died, they knew of our pain. Three days after Cowslip's death on that Sunday morning, our doorbell rang about 8 a.m. We went to the door and a courier was standing there with a large bouquet of roses. We were puzzled, but my wife took the flowers and then found the tiny card stuck in the bouquet. When she opened it, it read only, "In memory of Cowslip." Then—and only then—did the tears flow. Somebody knew. Somebody remembered. The flowers were from church folk miles away, but they were a gift from God.

The third Cowslip story was from a few days later. When Cowslip passed away, we were faced with where to bury her, and, honestly, there was no place to bury her. Our house was rented, and we discovered, much to our amazement, that there was no pet cemetery near us. We decided to wait. This was going to require more work and care than we thought. So we got Cowslip's favorite blanket, put her best kerchief on her, included some of her old toys, wrapped her carefully, and placed her in the only place we knew she would be, well, OK: in the freezer compartment of the refrigerator, which, not being big meat-eaters, we seldom used except for bird seed. As fortune would have it, my mother came for a holiday visit, and when we were away one afternoon she decided to fix dinner for us, drawing from the freezer a package that she assumed was some frozen meat. She carefully unwrapped it, at the same time heating up the skillet on the stove. Well, the rest of the story will have to wait for another time.

These are all stories from my stenographer's pad, summarized a bit. Every day something different, despite the recurrence of Cowslip stories. Some pieces in my notebook I will probably never use, others I have used already. But whenever I begin to prepare a sermon on a particular theme or topic, I turn to my story notebooks, looking for stories that will serve this particular topic or theme. What I become particularly aware of as I go through my story notebooks is that virtually every story that one finds and might use in a sermon must be very carefully unfolded and sensitively told. One must constantly ask oneself whose experiences might be left out if I tell this story, or if I tell this story in this particular way. Being sensitive to such a thing would probably not mean that one would omit the story, though on occasion that could be necessary; more often, though, such a sensitivity would let one set up and tell the story in a way that minimizes any alienation that a story might potentially create.

In addition, one must also stay very sensitive to the fact that certain stories, told in certain ways, might actually create pain within some who hear the story. For example, I would to be very careful in telling the story of our decision to place Cowslip's body in our freezer so that it not come across as callous or demeaning; I would want to tell it, in other words, as reflective of our profound love of Cowslip, so that someone who might recently have lost a beloved pet, too, might feel a sense of shared grief and dilemma with us, rather than feel I was making light in any way of the loss of our pet. These are all important matters, often overlooked in storytelling, matters that, by being downplayed, have tended to give storytelling a bad name in the pulpit. But storytelling in preaching today—and particularly in the comic sermon—is too important not to confront these issues forthrightly. When they are confronted, the preacher is given new power—and sensitivity—in the pulpit. Overall, the process of story collecting and recording, and storytelling, works. Even if the stories are not comic in nature, they become comic as they form a part of the sermon, just as Prof. Craddock's stories have in the sermon that we have examined here, and will look at in a different way later on.

One of the most difficult issues to be faced in storytelling, particularly in comic sermons, is whether the stories must be told "just as they happened." Is that a true story? is the question that often confronts the preacher after a sermon which contains a particularly funny or poignant story. The answer, by and large, is that, yes, it should be a true story. If the preacher tells it as "his" story or "her" story, then it *should* indeed be his or her story and no one else's. This is the issue of integrity or credibility again. But no story is ever told, no matter where or by whom, just as it happened. That is, in fact, probably an impossibility. The story is a recollection, a matter of selecting a structure, of selecting details of language and description, of shaping the pace and the movement of the story, of reconceiving its points of emphasis and even its perspective. The teller of the story gets to "tell" the story, making a myriad of decisions about *how* the story will be told. This, in fact, is the fun of storytelling; it is the power, even, of the storyteller's art. But the story, as true as it is, is always processed by the storyteller, and no two people who share the same story will ever tell it the same way.

Remembering Stories Differently

I tried an experiment about this a couple of years ago. I have a story, one that I remember vividly, that took place when I was about 13 and my younger brother John, now also a preacher and homiletician, was about 11. I was more athletic than John back then and one Sunday afternoon I and a group of my friends were playing baseball, and we would not let John play. He just wasn't good enough, we thought, for our brand of baseball. Our parents were away for a short time that afternoon, and John knew that someone in our church had given our dad some fireworks which he kept in a very prohibited bedroom drawer. Nevertheless, John decided to take revenge on me. He got into that drawer of dad's, found a cherry bomb, took one of my brand new shoes from our closet—I was very proud of my new cleat dress shoes—set the shoe on the sidewalk behind the house, put the cherry bomb under it and lit it. He blew my new shoe to smithereens. Boy, did he get into trouble. But I was still out my new pair of shoes.

A couple of years ago, I told that story—my story—to John and asked how he remembered the incident—I assumed he did; I wanted to know how he would tell the story of that hot Sunday afternoon. The story he told was remarkably different from mine. There was no revenge involved. He was not interested in playing baseball, and, instead, he was deeply curious about what kind of explosion a cherry bomb would make. He didn't think it would do much damage, and he thought my new shoe was thick enough to muffle any sound that the cherry bomb might make. He was not prepared for it to utterly destroy my new shoe. Whose story is true? The question is irrelevant. We fashion our stories to reflect how we process and re-create various experiences of our past; and even when our experiences overlap, our stories of those experiences seldom do. But that does not mean our stories are not true.

The issue, though, about truth in storytelling is more complex than this. Is it ever permissible in preaching to make up stories, to devise stories for the sake of what one wishes to say in a sermon? My inclination is to say yes, it is. Most of Jesus' parables appear to be made-up stories, once-upon-a-time stories. But there are also what we might call *stylized* stories—stories that we claim as our own, but that are clearly made up; and we simply "add" ourselves to the story. These are stories of our imagining. They are the storyteller "thinking up" a story. They are make-believe, even though we can often put ourselves squarely in the middle of such make-believe. People who hear such stories know what they are and what they are for. The stories often contain multiple clues about their make-believe qualities so that those who share the stories are not misled. One of the best examples of this kind of make-believe story that I have ever found in a sermon comes, again, from Fred Craddock, from "The Hard Side of Epiphany," a sermon that should not be a comic sermon, but it is; and it works. In the middle of the sermon, though, he makes up a story about himself, and he tells it this way:

> When first I entered the ministry—or was I dreaming, that's how it was, a dream of ministry at seventeen years old—I fantasticized the enemy. I loved the enemy. I idealized, I needed the enemy, because in my fantasies I was a martyr. I could lie on my little cot in summer camp beside the lake of Weeki-Weeki, or Noki-Noki, or whatever it was, and imagine what it would be like to give my life to Jesus Christ, because we'd sung that hymn around the lake that night, you know, holding candles. Are you able? Are you able? Are you able to drink the cup? Are you able? Are you able? I said yes, yes, yes. I'd lie up there in my bed in that dormitory and imagine I'm able to give my life for Jesus Christ. I could picture myself being boiled in a pot somewhere, frozen to death in the tundras of the North, stood before a gray wall early in the morning and someone saying, Do you believe Jesus is the Christ, the Son of God? Deny him and live.
>
> I'd say, I believe.
>
> Ready, aim, fire!
>
> Flags at half-mast, widows weeping in the afternoon— Oh, I fantasized. I needed Herod in those days. I needed an enemy. I needed opposition. Into the arena, king turns thumb down; the cage opens; in comes the lion to tear me apart; and a monument is erected: HERE'S WHERE FRED GAVE HIS LIFE. People come with their Polaroids: Stand over there, Charles. Let's get your picture next to the monument where old Fred gave his life. Boy, did I fantasize ministry.

Did that really happen? Is that a true story? No one who heard the sermon would mistake it for a real event. It is a stylized story, a story that, in the teller's mind and memory may be true—but true only in the sense that it sums up an attitude, a way of thinking about things then, a way of experiencing something. In a brilliantly comic way, it catches a mood of a teenage faith, the sense of what it meant "back then" to be a true believer. One could not express that mood or that sense of things in a didactic form, at least not with the degree of accuracy that a simple, concocted story is able to express it. It is a parody, really, of oneself, of the preacher. If there is a caution that must be exercised here, it is that in devising such stories one must never create stereotypes of other individuals or classes of people. Young preachers are prone to devise stories of "old people," those, they say, in their fifties and sixties. Older preachers are liable to talk about "kids," like those in their twenties and thirties. Such notions are age stereotypes, and one must stay away from them. One can be tempted to talk about "foreigners" as a stereotype or about those who like this or that, still in stereotypical mode.

Where did Craddock's Weeki-Weeki "story" come from? It came literally from the preacher's early experience, not because it happened that way, but because that is how the preacher reconstructed the mood of that time and embodied it in a colorful self-parody. It probably has its origin in a real event or a series of real events. The preacher as a youth was a camper, probably summer upon summer, a week at a time. There were the campfire experiences at whatever the name of that lake was. There were the sermons and the calls to missionary work. Those were all real; and the story in memory of those days is a distilled composite of how one at that age digested what was going on.

This is, in a sense, how all such stories from the past are remembered and told. Can one take a "real story" from one's past and re-create it for use in a particular sermon with a particular need and theme? That is not only what one can do in preaching, but what one often needs to do in order for the comic spirit to take form in sermonic storytelling. The sermon is not made, in other words, to serve one's stories. On the contrary—one's stories are made—literally made—to serve one's sermons. Stories must have detail, carefully crafted detail. They have to be set up with enough background to be vivid and to appeal to the imagination—as Craddock's Weeki-Weeki story does; yet they must also be unspecific enough to appeal to every congregant's imagination, as well as to the preacher's. Stories that go on too long, or that are too far-fetched, can drown a sermon. Yet a story that is concise and that rings true not only can light up a sermon, but can bring a gem of truth home in an unforgettable way.

If I return to my stenographer's pads, my story notes for piece upon piece that I have collected over a number of years, I thumb them with my sermon idea in mind. I find a story that is very close to what I think I need. I like it and want to use it. But it is not exactly right, at least not if I have to follow exactly what my notes tell me happened back then, whenever it was. So I decide to stylize my story, to fashion it—it is my story—to be of service to the sermon that I am preparing. I will shape the story's opening to fit where I wish it to be in the sermon. I will fill in details, some of which I may actually remember and decide to use, others which I will sketch to fit into both the tone and the texture of the sermon in which it will find its place. I am like a painter who has done a series of sketches and now in front of the canvas I must make placements of objects, not exactly where they were but where my composition best requires them to be; and I must select colors, not exactly as they were back then, but as I need them to be in order to create the kinds of color harmonies that will create for me the best painting possible. I am stylizing my painting to be a good painting, and I will stylize my story in order to maximize its contribution to the sermon in which it will be lodged. Moreover, I will shape the story's characters, and even its "ending," so that it ends up "saying" what I want it to say in the context of this sermon. Those are natural freedoms, artistic freedoms, ones that are necessary for the creation of a comic sermon.

The freedoms of storytelling, however, go even beyond this. We began this chapter by suggesting that the art of storytelling is the foundation of the comic sermon. This means that all of the other comic "tools" still to be discussed tend to work best when they are themselves incorporated within the context of a story. The other comic ingredients are stirred into the story mix. They become the means by which the comic process of storytelling becomes, if you please, comically-enhanced. Of course the other comic tools can be used in a variety of settings and forms, but they seem to work best when they are part of the art of storytelling. A stand-up comic can be funny telling an extended series of unrelated jokes, but the comedy lacks a certain intensity. When those same comic devices, however, are utilized within the context of a strong half-hour situation comedy such as *M*A*S*H* or *Frasier*, when they are used, that is, within what comedians call a sketch, the comic tools are themselves enhanced by being part of that larger comic context.

5

The Comic Premise:
Finding and Creating
Incongruities

If there is a principle that must be cultivated in order to activate consciously the comic spirit in the pulpit, it is the principle of incongruity. This is the principle of putting things together that do not go together, things that *should* not, by the normal modes of acting, go together. It is looking for one thing and getting something else. It is the odd juxtaposition between the real and the unreal, between the normal and the non-normal. It involves two "items"—two people, a person and a situation or object, two situations or two outlooks, two ideas or words, two of anything—two things that are diametrically opposed to each other, but which are forced to stand in the same place, forced to come to terms with each other. They are the basis for the comedy of "surprise": We sure didn't expect that. It is also the comic principle by which we learn to see old things in new ways, which is why Kenneth Burke has referred to comic creativity as "perspective by incongruity." It is also, in many ways, the playful way in which human creativity itself works. Creativity is essentially comic.

One finds this principle behind the comedy of virtually every medium and comic art form, whether past or present. We probably know it best as the fundamental premise behind television and film comedy, even though it can be conjured up in a variety of ways, many of them purely verbal—as in "stand-up" comedy—and it can certainly be adapted, via storytelling, to the "art" of the pulpit. Here our task will be to explain and illustrate the several forms that incongruity takes in classic comedy, including the classic forms of our own time. In addition, though, we will also explore one of the major ways in which professional comics actually generate their incongruous stories; and, in so doing, we shall appropriate that comedic process for the pulpit. First, though, we will consider the various forms of comic incongruity, "tried and true" forms, but ones that, when creatively explored in novel, imaginative ways, still provide the freshest and funniest of human comedy.

A first form of comic incongruity is that found between *the anticipated and the unanticipated*. Life is, by and large, lived in patterns, patterns and habits that keep us sane and relatively safe. We know what to expect, generally, from one moment to the next. We learn what we can expect from people, from things, even from situations. We depend on those expectations. It is when those expectations get interrupted in some cockeyed, even jolting, fashion that the comic possibilities emerge. Granted, some interruptions may not be comic at all; in fact, they may be tragic. And yet, when those interruptions are relatively safe, when they are not mortally threatening, when they cause us to look at ourselves, at others, at our situations and patterns of life differently, then those interruptions become the genius of the comic. They become the basis, in fact, of all great comic storytelling: "You should have seen what happened to my wife the other day. She was on her way to work, driving down the highway as she always does when suddenly…" and there the comic story, after a few moments of normal routine set-up, kicks in; and it kicks in with the unexpected, the unanticipated.

Earlier, in our discussion of storytelling, I suggested that one learn to keep a daily (evening) journal of some real story-experiences from every day. Here is the key for what to look for in one's story recording. One looks for something that happened that was *unexpected*. In the midst of one's routines, of going about one's business as one does day in and day out, where were the unanticipated interruptions? Where were the moments, the events, when the anticipated and the unanticipated clashed? As I said a few moments ago, sometimes such interruptions are not comic; and, in fact, often they are not fun. They interrupt the flow of safe and sane activity and must somehow be dealt with, as they invariably will be. But what also often happens is that, in retrospect, those interrupted moments *become* comic events. The unanticipated may not have been funny at the time—it may have been too inconvenient or perplexing—but afterward it has a way of showing its comic dimensions. Those can become, in fact, the best stories that one ends up telling.

Ambition vs. Achievement

A second classic pattern of comic incongruity is that between *human ambition and human achievement.* Just saying this, however, does little justice to the enormous range of comic expression buried under this simple idea. At its most obvious level, this represents the comedy of one who wants to be a particular thing, but is constantly frustrated in his or her best, unrelenting efforts to be whatever that is. This is the comedy of one who wishes to be a great singer or, say, a violinist, but who has virtually no talent or native inclination to support that ambition. In American comedy, it was Jack Benny, always there with his violin, who wanted to perform and who surrounded himself with all of the trappings and poses of one who would and could perform on the violin, yet no one ever heard him play. I don't know if he could actually play or not, but much of his comedy lay in the juxtaposition, the incongruity, between his unrepentant ambition and his never playing in public, despite his ever-present violin.

One may look anywhere and everywhere in comedy for the playing out of this principle. It is at the heart of Charlie Chaplin's comedy, carried out in such thoroughly visual fashion. Charlie's ambitions were unfailing, usually his ambitions with women, but there were also his vocational ambitions. And while every now and then he would seem to have some success, in the end, he was always thwarted in some way; he was, after all, forever the little tramp, despite the dignity that he always maintained in his trampness. Whenever one watches an early film comedy, in some way the clash is invariably between ambition—yes, I can do that, or we can do that—and achievement: we tried our best, but it didn't work out; and the comedy was always located in the profoundly serious, but always funny, incongruity between those two underlying notions.

In episode after episode of *I Love Lucy*, which will probably be seen forever in reruns, the principle is unfailing as Lucy's ambitions forever outstrip her abilities. Granted, there are innumerable other comic devices operative in those unforgettable shows, but the comic "story" of each show is based in the incongruity between what she wants and what she will get. (It is hard to know whether to speak in the past tense or the present tense here.) In the famous episode in the candy factory where Lucy and Ethel go to work on the "simple" job of wrapping the candy on the conveyer belt, what they think they can do is quickly outstripped by the circumstances that make it harder and harder to do what the job calls for. It is easy at first and there is no comedy there; they do what they are supposed to do. But then the conveyer belt speeds up, and speeds up, and they are faced with their abilities being left behind by the demands of the job. It is simple to state the premise, but when it is acted out it creates uproarious comedy as Lucy and Ethel are forced to cope with the gap between what they were expected to do on the candy line and what it turns out that they actually can do. Think about episode after episode of Lucy and one finds this comic premise underlying whatever the plot is.

In contemporary television, even a sophisticated situation comedy like *Frasier* is based, at its most fundamental level, on the *conflict between desire and achievement*. Both Frasier and Niles are psychiatrists, highly trained as problem-solvers, both passionately committed to helping people cope with their neuroses, phobias, and hang-ups. Yet, in episode after episode, both of them prove resolutely inept, not only at solving other people's problems—which Frasier tries to do over the radio—but even in dealing with their own overflowing neuroses, phobias, and hang-ups. Niles, who counsels others on marriage problems, carries out a dysfunctional, on-again, off-again marriage of pathetic proportions with Maris; and Frasier, who is ever desirous of female "conquests," reminiscent even of Sam back at the Cheers bar, never succeeds, even though in episode after episode he comes perilously close. The comedy in all of this is found in that wondrous and unfailing gap between ambition and achievement.

In another sense, this is James Thurber's character of Walter Mitty—it is a Walter Mitty principle—in which one lives in a real world of common everydayness, but in one's heart one lives another life, a "secret" life, one that will remain forever an exalted, imaginary life. It is Snoopy the dog, living forever on top of his doghouse, but in his imagination, he is forever the World War II Flying Ace who is perpetually surrounded by adoring fans, preferably female fans.

The Ideal and the Actual

A third incongruity on which the comic spirit often rests is between *the ideal and the actual*. This is related, of course, to both of the earlier forms of incongruity, but it is often quite different in the way in which it is played out. This is the principle that underlies such comic visions as *The Wizard of Oz*, where the ideal is symbolized by the Great City at the end of the Yellow Brick Road. It is where the Wizard lives, the Great and Powerful Wizard. We develop ideals, things that call to us and motivate us, things large and small—and the small ones are often the most comic when we bring them to consciousness. But when we get to the end of the Yellow Brick Road—today, tomorrow, someday—what we find is just some silly old man, a bumbler who is no wizard at all; he is just someone with a tiny bit of wisdom, a lot of laughter, and a few homemade badges to stick on people's shirts. When this is played out in various artistic forms—including the pulpit—it is a bittersweet kind of comedy, but it is comic, nonetheless, and often our laughter gets mixed with tears. We want our ideals to be big things; we construct them as large as possible and set them out in front of us to call to us and pull us; and yet, in actuality, they are never what we think they are. And the comedy is, again, in that incongruous gap.

In my reflection on the classic *M*A*S*H* television series—I once taught a graduate communication seminar at Pepperdine University on the comedy of *M*A*S*H*—this seems to me to have been its guiding comic premise. This is why, unlike most television comic sitcoms, *M*A*S*H* was as sad as it was funny, something that seems often to be the case with this particular incongruity. It was comedy, pure and simple, often slapstick in its style; and yet seldom an episode went by but that tears were brought to the surface, not in a cheap fashion, but real tears for real human situations, which was the genius of the work. Even the set-ups of the program tapped this incongruity. The operating "rooms" conjured up the comic gap between the ideal and the actual. One was forced to think: These are operating rooms?! Everything in the operating rooms was jerry-rigged, and much of the comedy was in how things were done and in the weird ingenuities that had to make life-saving devices out of paper clips, string, and surplus toilet seats, or whatever. So many other elements also played into this incongruity. For example, Hawkeye's drink of choice, his martinis, were made of who-knows-what in some mysterious still that seems to have been under his cot. He's drinking what? Many elements of characterization and visualization contributed to *M*A*S*H*'s great comedic impact, but at its base was the fundamental incongruity between the ideals of surgery and saving lives and the actualities of doing so in the primitive conditions of a fictitious place.

Individual vs. Institution

A fourth incongruity that underlies the comedic spirit is that between *the individual and an institution*, between a person and a giant bureaucracy, the isolated person and the system. This "clash" is often combined with one of those that we have just discussed for its full comic effect; for example, one's ideals continuously thwarted by the overpowering, impersonal bureaucracy or one's ambitions never achieved as a result of one's resources being continually drained by the tax machine or by some conniving boss at the top of the bureaucratic heap. Yet, more directly, stories of bureaucratic entanglements, of an individual fighting and fighting and fighting the "system," are also comic in and of themselves. One gets on the telephone to complain about some particular thing, or to get some small screw-up straightened out by, say, the telephone company, and then the fun begins. From getting nothing but answering machines and being told to punch number after number into the phone, all to little avail, to getting a person who is the wrong person who transfers you to another person who is also the wrong person who transfers you to yet another person who is almost the right person, and so one—the comic imagination can do a great deal with such an incongruity.

The Normal and the Abnormal

There is a fifth basic form of comic incongruity, one that often underlies motion pictures, but one that can also, in story form, be utilized in verbal ways as well. It is the process of setting what we might call the *normal* in juxtaposition with the *abnormal*. Such terms are not meant to be pejorative in any way; nor are they meant to hang us up on the question of what or who is normal or abnormal. Usually this incongruity means that one sets an abnormal person in a normal world, or the reverse in which a normal person is set in the midst of an abnormal world. This is the comic incongruity behind Dustin Hoffman's *Tootsie*—with Hoffman's Michael Dorsey becoming Dorothy Michaels, a man trying to function in a woman's world in order to get an acting job in a soap opera. The work world is normal, as it were, but Hoffman assumes an abnormal character trying to function in that world. The comedy plays itself through with the incongruities that such a charade necessitates. The same premise created a fresh movie as well in Robin Williams' *Mrs. Doubtfire,* that premise being an abnormal individual, or an abnormally-functioning individual, living in and coping with a very normal world. The same premise, moreover, handled in very different ways, provided the mainspring for movies such as *Big*, in which Tom Hanks was an adult—or an adult body—forced to live in a child's normal world. Even *Forest Gump* was based on this incongruity, with Hanks, again, portraying an "abnormal" person in a normal world; the unique genius of this award-winning movie was that it had Forest Gump going from one kind of abnormality early on to a very different, and surprising, abnormality as the story progressed. It was all brilliantly and very comically done.

One can turn this around as well—though it does not happen as often—and think of comic movies and sitcoms in which a normal person is placed in an abnormal world, and the comic gap takes a different form. This is the basis, for example, for stories that place individuals in cultures or surroundings that are not their own, facing characters and situations with which they are unfamiliar. It is the basis for the comedy of sending a "common" person to Washington's wild and weird political world. It is the basis for sending ordinary city folk to live in the country, as the *Green Acres* television series did. It is the basis for sending ordinary country folk to live in Beverly Hills, as the *Beverly Hillbillies* did, even though now we are getting confused as to which world is normal and which is abnormal. But the premise invariably works to create striking comedic situations.

There are, of course, other possible incongruities on which the comic vision rests, of which these are only a few. These, in fact, can be twisted and turned and configured in an endless number of directions to create comic juxtaposition or incongruity. What should be noted is that when setting up these incongruities, whether in television, in film, or even in storytelling, it is not just comedy that results, whatever the nature of the comedy. As Burke would remind us, *such incongruities also set up new ways of seeing the world and ourselves in it*. More than laughs are at stake, though the comedy is certainly tied up with this process. What is also at stake is the use of the comic vision to create new "perspectives," new, fresh ways of seeing, thinking, and experiencing. That is why, in short, such notions are, or should be, very much a part of the process of Christian preaching.

The Newspaper and Incongruities

Having said all this, however, about the nature or mainspring of the comic process, the question is how to relate these matters to sermon-making. One does it in two basic ways—in storytelling as part of the sermon and by finding materials in the world around us from which the incongruities of life can be both found and fashioned. We have already examined the storytelling process, and what we have said in this chapter about incongruity can easily be incorporated into our stories. The second way, though, will be taken up here. It involves the same process, or processes, that are used over and over again by virtually all professional stand-up comedians, from Johnny Carson and Jay Leno in their opening televised "monologues" to the comics of the comedy club circuits. It involves what is often called topical comedy or humor, the comedy of incongruity that arises from the daily newspaper.

This calls for the preacher to become an inveterate newspaper reader, a paper a day at the start of the day is what I press my students to turn into a habit. The preacher, moreover, reads the paper with a pair of scissors in hand, creating what will be an always-growing clip file. It will be the comic clip file, not for this week or next necessarily—in fact, with nothing particularly in mind at the time—but clippings to which one can always return, usually on a weekly basis. For the comic clip file, one is looking for stories that reflect the kinds of incongruities that we have noted so far—any kinds of incongruities. In the process of reading and clipping, one is not asking what will I use this or that for; one is only saving, knowing that there is a chance of coming back to this or that piece at some point in the future. Anyone who has watched late-night talk shows knows that the writers for those host-comics would each day comb the newspaper—the "what's in the news today?" line became a staple of Johnny Carson's monologues—and they would clip strange bits and stories. Often they would simply re-tell the real stories, emphasizing their comic, or incongruous, aspects; at other times they would devise comic observations and quip lines, gags, or story twists, often with points attached to them, from those news stories. Since it is topical humor, the materials can be used even though the news stories may be weeks or even months old, involving no more, usually, than the filling in of some details bring the news "event" back, whether it is remembered or not.

I still try to keep a working newspaper clip file, one from which comedic stories can be drawn for use in my sermons. As I go through it now, I will indicate a few of the stories that I have recently lifted, and even though I have not used any of them yet in a sermon, I think I know under what kinds of circumstances I would; and I can already tell something of the humor that might be possible with each one.[1]

1. I clipped a front-page news story about the Food and Drug Administration approving a new treatment for male baldness, since I am one of those men who, if not actually concerned about the nature of my being "follically-challenged," is at least interested in the gradual disappearance of my hair. The story begins:

> The oldest-known prescription was an Egyptian concoction for treating hair loss.
> Now, as the world counts down to the third millennium, the latest prescription also promises a cure for baldness. The Food and Drug Administration announced Monday that it approved Propecia, the first pill for male pattern baldness, which offers the potential for men to grow new hair and stop existing strands from falling out.
> The pill, developed by Merck and Co., is supposed to help men regrow lost hair—but the drug might be of far greater benefit inside the head than on top, say those familiar with the psychology of baldness.
> An estimated 33 million American men have male pattern baldness, characterized by a receding hair line and hair loss at the crown of the scalp. One survey, published four years ago in a dermatology journal, found that more than

90 percent of men who were growing bald worried about the future of their hair.

Well, enough. I clipped the entire story, and it is a beaut from beginning to end. As far as comic incongruity is concerned, I think we are dealing here (hair?) with the incongruity between the ideal and the actual, between what we men might really want to take place, even desperately want to take place, and what will actually, ever, take place. Or it might be seen as a juxtaposition between one's ambition and one's achievement. One wants to grow hair, or at least be able to hang onto the hair one has, for as long as possible; and yet one knows—as most men know down deep—that once the hair starts to go there is really very little that anybody or anything can do about it. But the desire to reverse that process in some way never goes away, at least not for most of us, and I wonder about the truthfulness of the rest.

Now, professional comedy writers could no doubt come up with some clever repartee based on this news story or even some very funny punch line, a twist on the story itself perhaps. But one does not have to be a professional, or even a particularly clever, comedy writer to see the joy of humor that oozes from this story. It is a serious story, of course, and men who are worried about hair loss are serious about their hair loss. But it all has a very funny side to it, too, as most balding men are the first to point out. For me, the comic side of it is in what we might call the constancy of hope, hope that, as they say, springs eternal. The human spirit—the male spirit in this case—never gives up. Whenever a new prescription comes along, the hope is renewed, revived, and when the FDA, the federal government of the United States of America gets involved, that represents the highest form of hope that can light one's fires anew. Never mind that the FDA is itself probably run by a bunch of aging bureaucrats, many of whom suffer, I suspect, from severe male pattern baldness. This is a news story that I will be able to use someday, in some sermon. I will file it away, under the heading of "hope," no doubt.

2. On a very different note, I clipped this story; perhaps you saw it and remember it as well:

> A mother who took her son to see a shopping center Santa Claus recognized the jolly old soul as her ex-husband and slapped him with court papers branding him a deadbeat dad.

"Daddy is Santa!" the little boy exclaimed during last month's confrontation in a Brooklyn mall. LaToya Ramirez said she reached into her purse and handed Neil Ramirez court papers that claim he had failed to pay child support since July 1.

"He put them in his sack," she said…A few days later, Ramirez returned to the shopping center and again confronted "St. Nick." She said he poked her in the chest and then she pummeled him. Ramirez said he never touched his ex-wife, but conceded children were screaming, "She's beating up Santa Claus!"

What a story, even though it goes on for another dozen or so paragraphs. One cannot make up a story like that. For all of its seriousness, it has comedy written all over it. This is a story that can be told in a sermon, told as the newspaper told it. It is a kind of ultimate juxtaposition at several levels. It contains the incongruity of playing Santa for hundreds of children while ignoring one's own children, the incongruity of what we have called the unanticipated, in this case of taking the children to see Santa and discovering the missing dad behind the Santa suit. One not only can tell this story, but one can "play" with it. The real humor in this story, in fact, might well be in trying to describe all of this happening from the viewpoint of a child, a child that really does believe in Santa Claus. Now that is a serious incongruity, packed with possibilities. Unfortunately, I do not have the time right now to unpack those possibilities, but what I can see at the moment is that the story enables one, in a comic fashion, to talk about the dangers of too much make-believe, of trying to "pretend" to be things that we are not, whatever our motives might be. Just when we think we are Santa Claus, and a pretty good one at that, someone comes along to slap us with, well, court papers. There are other possibilities here that a preacher's good imagination will not fail to find.

3. I also clipped a story from Ottawa, Canada, about a member of the Canadian Senate, a very strange story indeed, one with comic possibilities:

He's shown up for work just fourteen times in seven years—and then only to fill out the necessary paperwork to continue drawing his annual $60,000 in pay and other financial perks from Canadian taxpayers.

Then, heigh-ho, it's back to a palatial residence in Mexico's Baja California, where Sen. Andrew Thompson, 73, resides for most of the year. It is a lifestyle he has enjoyed ever since landing a seat in Canada's Senate in 1967. But Thompson's colleagues in this country's most ridiculed political institution have finally decided enough is enough. After months of dithering, senators last week took tough action. Sort of. They voted to strip him of the secretary he never uses and the office suite he never occupies. But he is still a senator and still collects his salary.

"This measure shows we can take stern measures, if need be," said Sen. Anne Cools of Ontario. "I say, 'Hooray for us!'"

It is a slapstick news story, if ever there was one. Is this for real? Is this in the real world? Stern measures? Sen. Cools only adds to the fun of it all. It is not easy to know what kind of comic incongruity is at work here. It is probably the comedy of juxtaposing expectation—i.e., the fact that old Sen. Thompson would actually serve in the Senate—and the actuality—i.e., that he has never had any intention of serving in the Senate, despite getting paid to do just that. My initial inclination would be to utilize this story to talk about the demands that are actually made on all of us "working stiffs," male and female, in the real world. One could have some real fun with the story of Sen. Thompson. Let's say that we used his approach to "work" in any of our lives, in the life, say, of you there in the third pew who works as a plumber for a respected plumbing firm in town. You show up at the office to sign your papers, to make sure your payroll withholding and deduction forms are in order, and then twice a month you stop by to pick up your paycheck. But on those in-between days, you take the RV and go on various fishing trips, first up North, then out to Nevada, and then—down to Baja in Mexico, where you fish alongside your friend, Andy Thompson who, as far as you can tell, is from someplace up in Canada. Would your job go as well as his? What would happen to you? These are simple points, simple matters, and there are places in sermons for handling such issues. But a good comic story, one like the Sen. Thompson story, provides a highly comic framework in which to deal with such things.

4. That same newspaper, from December 23rd, carried another story that I clipped, a little piece tucked away in the back. It was

from Oslo, Norway, via the Associated Press. Here is what the story said:

> The search for the perfect Christmas tree went a little too far for one Norwegian family, who became lost in the deep forest overnight. A 34-year-old father, his 12-year-old daughter, 10-year-old son and the family dog set out Sunday from the southern town of Raelingen to cut a tree. When they failed to return, at least 80 searchers headed into the hills to find them, the Norwegian state radio network reported. They were discovered about 11 a.m. Monday, after nearly 24 hours in sub-freezing temperatures. "They were cold and tired but otherwise in reasonably good shape," said police spokesman Asbjoern Gran. "They huddled together and used the German Shepherd to help keep warm. They didn't get much sleep. They also didn't get a Christmas tree."

A strange and innocuous little story, to be sure, but it caught my eye. It has comic possibilities, not just in its telling, but in its elaboration, in its pathos. It is the kind of piece from which a *M*A*S*H*-like story could be developed. One could create from the story, using imagination and empathetic grace. The incongruity is in the joy of a probably much-anticipated activity—the finding and cutting of this year's Christmas tree—and the pain of getting lost on a very cold night, and ending up with nothing. It is anticipation juxtaposed with the unanticipated. This is an example of a story of an event that, at the time it was lived, was harsh and frightening, but that probably will become funny, even for its participants, as it is told again and again, a story of the "you'll never guess what happened to us" kind.

5. I am a long-time country music fan, used to play it in my disc jockey days on the radio back in Illinois, so I was quite taken with a little news story, again buried in the back of the newspaper. I clipped it; here it is:

> President Clinton reportedly plans to nominate Country Music Foundation director William Ivey as the new chairman of the National Endowment for the Arts. "This is a particularly important agency, particularly in its role nurturning excellence in all the arts," Ivey told the Washington Post. The Post said the White House has settled on Ivey to replace Jane Alexander at the NEA's helm.

That's it; that was the article. I am aware that the piece says the president is "planning" to nominate Mr. Ivey. What I want to know is where do I write to vote for his getting the appointment done just as soon as possible? It seems to me that this country, whatever one thinks of Bill Clinton, might be headed in the right direction after all. A country music person as head of the entire US of A arts establishment. Think of that. What possibilities! That means that Mr. Ivey would have a good deal of influence not only with the President, but on Capitol Hill, doesn't it? With those senators and representatives? If Mr. Ivey is as dyed-in-the-wool a country music person as I hope he is, as he appears to be, we might actually get some of that country flavor in, well, all of the highfalutin arts, mightn't we? Just wondering. The little story has some comic possibilities, at least it does from where I sit, and from which I preach. The juxtaposition, the incongruity is between those two worlds—the world of Nashville and the world of Washington. I realize that country music performers like Dolly Parton and Johnny Cash have performed at the White House and even at those tuxedo balls in downtown Washington, but a high-ranking country music bureaucrat? Imagine that. What I don't know, though, is whether this amounts to putting an abnormal individual into a normal setting or a normal individual into an abnormal setting. It's worth thinking about. It has comic possibilities.

6. About the same time I also clipped a column from a local columnist whose work I like. This is not an opinion column as such—I would stay away from those—but it is a reportorial column, and I like what he wrote about. He was discussing all of the catalogues that arrive all year long, but particularly just before the holidays. Every company has its catalogue, and they all want to get them into your hands. But he got down, then, to a catalogue he had read about and had to send away for, the official catalogue of Skeletons in the Closet, the—yes—the gift shop of the Los Angeles Coroner's Office. The column continued:

> It is not a thick catalogue, and there are a few notable themes. Many items, including beach towels, coffee mugs, Post-It pads, visors, etc., feature the familiar chalk-traced body logo. (It's a unisex body in a prone position.) Weary retailers might appreciate a sign with an unusually aggressive tone: "Shoplifters' Next of Kin Will Be Notified." Or, "Checks Accepted With Two Forms of I.D. or Dental Records." (Each sign is just $10.)

Another theme that resonates throughout the catalogue is the tried-and-true toe tag. The toe-tag key chain ($5) includes a blue plastic card inscribed, "This could be you. Please don't drink and drive." (Inscription can be personalized.) There is a "Foot with toe tag lapel pin" and a lovely toe-tag T-shirt.

Well, I clipped the entire column, but underlined the part about the Sketetons in the Closet gift shop catalogue. Since then, I have ordered my own copy. If ever I make use of this catalogue in a sermon, I must credit my friend the columnist, of course, for putting me on to it, but I will make the use of it in a sermon quite my own—which will not be difficult to do, now that I have seen the catalogue itself. Comedically, it rests on the incongruity between the expected and the unexpected. It is about catalogues. We all know the catalogues, from Gurney's seed books to all of the museum and public TV related things, from the junk catalogues to the very specialized ones, like music catalogues and cold weather wear catalogues and even those underwear ones. But then along comes one that is unexpected, that seems to tap into a different kind of psyche. Or, as the Coroner's Office catalogue puts it, "Part of you thinks it's in poor taste, while part of you wants an XL." It is out of sync. It is not what we expect. Its humor is in that unexpectedness, that element of maudlin surprise.

I have only scratched the surface of my newspaper clip file. What should be clear in thinking through this process is that it is not that one looks for, and finds, things that are naturally funny. That, in fact, is usually not the case, despite the note I found about the Skeletons in the Closet catalogue. In most cases, one finds news stories that are news stories because they are incongruous, because they are "out of the ordinary." All of this is only a way of opening up the fundamental comic premise and, in a sense, inviting it into the pulpit. This is not easy to do, of course, and the preacher must undertake it with the greatest sense of caution and care. One should start, not by trying to create incongruity (which eventually can be done), but by finding incongruities in the columns of the daily newspaper, as we have suggested. Two things should be kept in mind, though, as one does this. First, one builds a clip file, not for the use of this particular piece or that one, but because one needs a collection from which to draw when the need arises. In other words, the sermon idea—whether the idea *for* the sermon or an idea *within* a particular sermon—comes first; it must come first. It will be some incongruency of scripture versus behavior, of ethic believed versus lived, or two behaviors in conflict, whatever, and then one will turn to one's file to see if there might be a story of comic incongruity from the news that can help light up, or give form to, that particular idea. One does not, in other words, start with a good newspaper story and try to figure out how to use it in a sermon. That simply will not work.

The second thing to remember is that one uses a newspaper story just as it is, simply described, not wildly embellished or exaggerated. Usually such pieces speak for themselves when they are described: "Perhaps you saw this little story in last week's newspaper about— It said—Here, let me read you a few lines from it"; and then one focuses on a statement about its incongruity, letting that incongruity spill back into what one is talking about in the sermon. One must not assume too much, since congregants are listening to the story read and told, and not actually reading it themselves. So the preacher must make sure that it is filled in, and that the connections to the sermon are actually made and allowed to stand on their own as comic bits.

Hyperbole and Language

There are two other forms of incongruity that professional comedians often use and that are also available to the preacher, even though one must advise great caution in their use. One is the comedy of hyperbole, or exaggeration. Sometimes this is treated separately in studies of the comedic, but it is a variation of the incongruous. It, too, is a form of violating the expected, of expecting a particular way of talking, or of describing something and getting a very different, highly exaggerated way of talking or describing. Few comics are better at this, or better known for doing this, than Dave Barry, whose numerous books have been culled from his weekly newspaper columns. Barry manages to create a potent form of humor about the little things in life, things around the house, things from the simple days of growing up—and he does so by working some form of exaggeration into virtually every line he writes.

Recently, in his Christmas column, Barry described the happy days of childhood "racing down the stairs on Christmas morning to see what Santa Claus had brought. It felt like a dream," he said. "In fact, it was a dream, because I lived in a ranch-style home that did not have stairs." Sometimes, he said, Santa would bring a shiny new bicycle "with many shiny new unassembled parts lying on the floor where my father had abandoned them at

4:30 a.m. after giving up on trying to understand the instructions (STEP 143: Insert $3/16$" hexagonal toggle truncheon clockwise into camber gasket and tighten mortise nut until your hand bleeds)." Sometimes, Barry continued,

> Santa brought me a model-airplane kit consisting of a tube of cement and 576,000 plastic parts, every single one labeled "strut." It took a lot of time and patience, but if you followed the directions carefully, you could assemble these parts into an incredibly detailed, realistic-looking plane that seemed ready to soar into the sky. Notice I say you could do this. I always ended up with what looked like a large mutant dung beetle, permanently bonded to my desk by lumps of dried cement the size of walnuts.

With that, Barry is just getting warmed up. His comic shtick is exaggeration, line upon line, image upon image. You expect description and storytelling. You get ridiculously skewed description and storytelling. The problem with this kind of comedy is that it is very difficult to pull off. Barry's ability with it is both uncanny and unusual. One cannot imitate what he does, at least not regularly, though one does get a sense of how effective exaggeration can be as a comic tool.

A final kind of incongruity on which much comedy rests is that which involves word play; it, too, is a kind of comedy available to the preacher, even though it must be used sparingly and with great caution, too. At its lowest level is the art of punning, which uses a word with an "expected" meaning but sets the word into a setting that shifts the word's meaning to something not expected. The old example is the line about a man walking up to me on the street and saying that he had not had a bite in a week; so I bit him. It is, in many ways, an obvious and cheap form of humor, so cheap, in fact, that we often groan at puns instead of laughing at them. At its most sophisticated level, this is also the comedy of someone like George Carlin, the tough-minded, no-nonsense scrutinizer-of-language, whose career arose from the 1960s. One of Carlin's staples was, and is, taking commonly used terms and subjecting them to careful, literal scrutiny. When that is done, the term often means something quite different from the way it is actually used; and therein lies the unexpected, the incongruous, the humorous. This, though, can be done by preachers who can ask what we "mean" when we say such-and-such.

Do we really mean what we think we mean? If one can get by the blueness of his work, a trip with Carlin down this comic street can be most instructive.

While the story is the fundamental form of the comic spirit, incongruity (which is another, less baggage-laden term, for irony) is the fundamental premise of the comic spirit. And there are numerous ways that it can be utilized in preaching. Not to take over the pulpit by any means. If that happens, all of us who care about the gospel will crash and burn. But we know what is funny; we know how to find it and even create it. And if we can put it to the service of the pulpit, if we can demonstrate not only the joy of laughter that it conjures up, but use it as a way to hold up a mirror to our own silliness and even weirdness, then it will amplify the gospel and not diminish it. If we can laugh at our human incongruencies, there may actually be hope for us—not that we shall ever put an end to them, but that we might actually be able to come to terms with just how frail and human we really are.

6

The Comic Metaphor: Discovering What is What

One of the central ingredients of the comic sermon is the special form of incongruity that we know as the metaphor. Even though they are not particularly interested in its comedic dimensions, theologians and biblical scholars spend considerable effort today speculating about and investigating the nature of metaphor. This is largely because the New Testament and the Gospels in particular are saturated with it. Homileticians, too, are concerned with metaphor, though they usually call the metaphor an "image" or imagistic language. There is no desire here to attempt any contribution to, or even comment upon, the scholarship that currently surrounds metaphorical theory. Instead, here we shall return to the basics of metaphor, taking the term to mean what every good English teacher has taught for generations. A metaphor is a figure of speech used to explain something unfamiliar by something familiar. It is used to say that something is like something else; or, more precisely, that something *is* something else.

The metaphor is, without question, one of the most interesting and important ingredients in the comic arsenal. Good metaphor packs the wallop of incongruity and surprise. When it works, it is both profoundly insightful and funny at the same time, something that only the very best comic spirit can hope for. Achieving it requires a vivid comic imagination. Even though a great deal of theological study now surrounds the nature of metaphor in biblical text, very little direct study of it has gone on in homiletical circles; this means that preachers have been given relatively little help in grasping the special joys and delights that occur when metaphor is used in the creation of a comic sermon.

This does not mean that contemporary preachers do not know about what is usually called imagistic language. Such language is usually thought, though, to be a consequence of the MTV-like visuals of the contemporary television generation, so that it becomes preaching described by one homiletician as "increasingly visual in its imagery and imagistic in its content." Such a comment, however, is often set in a negative context. This homiletician, echoing well what several others have also voiced, added that such sermons "filled with an overly rich diet of imagery" result in the hearers, being "boggled and confused":

> Part of the problem was the expectation we hearers brought to the event—we came expecting some sequence of thoughts that we could follow, some plottable logic. That expectation, clearly, was denied. However, we also were left with a mood, an attitude, a certain state of affairs.
>
> After one such sermon, I remember that we hearers felt keenly the confused tumble of the images such as they assault us through the visual media; we had been inundated with the good, the bad, and the ugly, all coming at us at once. How we were to interpret this potpourri was not addressed in the sermon. Insofar as preachers are called to frame the images of our contemporary world in biblical terms, however, this particular sermon was a failure.[1]

Indeed, it sounds as though it was. Such cautions, without question, are well taken. There is a problem, however, that often appears in homiletical writing, and it is the confusing of so-called "imagistic" language and "figurative" language, such as metaphor. They are not the same thing, as most every undergraduate course in creative writing tries to make clear. Imagistic writing is vivid, visual writing. It is the use of language to create detailed, vibrant pictures in one's head. It is language designed to let the reader "see" what the writer sees or has seen. It is writing with color and sensuality, writing designed to take a reader to specific times and places, writing designed to create a sense of "being there." Imagistic writing (or speaking, as in the sermon) does not permit generalized adjectives like "beautiful" or "wonderful" or "horrible." Its adjectives are as precise and graphic as possible: fresh, accurate, and visual. Verbs are filled with verve and action; they are alive, not passive, limp, and hackneyed. Adverbs are subtle and polished, carefully nuanced. It is writing (or speaking) that is deeply involving by its very vividness. Can such imagistic writing be overdone? Of course it can. But then it is simply bad writing, too flowery, too packed, often too ostentatious. Ironically, good imagistic writing is usually done very sparingly and often with understatement, with precise words, carefully chosen. Such writing depends on fresh, visual details, not a rush of words.

Metaphor and Image

Metaphor, on the other hand, is not a descriptive device, not a form of visual language. Instead, it is an *explanatory* device, represented by language that must be explored and opened up in the writing or the speaking when it is used. Metaphor is not for the purpose of creating a picture, but of understanding; and the difference is crucial. True, imagery and metaphor, along with other kinds of figurative language, can be mixed together in any piece of work; but the creator of the work—the preacher creating the sermon, in this case—must be clear about the different roles that these different kinds of language play. The metaphor comes into use when an idea or a concept is too old or too abstract or too esoteric, when it is difficult to explain or bring to life. At that point, something familiar and concrete is summoned up, something that is said to "be like" that concept. It is never an exact likeness; it cannot be, which is why the metaphor, the new "object," usually must be explored if it is to do its work. But it is—or should be—enough like the original concept or notion to give it meaning, texture, and usability. And when the metaphor itself is fresh and new, then the old concept or idea itself becomes fresh and new. It is also true that if the metaphor is worn and threadbare, then the old concept will probably become, if it is not already, worn and threadbare as well.

One should now be able to see that the metaphor is perfectly positioned to become a prime comic device. By its nature, it involves two things set in juxtaposition: an old or difficult idea or concept and a new something, whatever that is. And if that new something is unexpected, then the comic spirit is set in motion; if it is incongruent and surprising, then exploring the metaphor becomes, itself, a comic event—an enlightening one, particularly if the metaphor is well chosen, but a comic one, nevertheless.

Something else should be said about the metaphor before we explore its role in the comic sermon. It is that there is no such thing as metaphorical language as opposed to "regular" or "normal" language. As any good writer knows, such a distinction just doesn't hold. Metaphor is a *function* of language, not a *substantive* part of a language system. This means that anything—literally anything—in language can become a metaphor, if the writer or speaker chooses to make it one. And one makes it one by investing it with meaning beyond what it normally possesses. A tree is a tree, and it could be described in detail, with its thick, leaf-padded branches arching outward and upward, turning it into an ornate green ball sitting on a heavy, dark pillar. You can see it if the words are "imaged" creatively. But this tree can be more than a tree, no matter how it is visualized, if the writer or speaker wants it to be more than a tree. It can be a metaphor. Only the speaker or writer can determine for what it will serve as a metaphor. It can be a metaphor for the tradition of Christian faith, let us say, something that is certainly difficult to "describe." So let this tree be that "tradition" by saying that it is. But it will require more than our just saying that it is. It will require elaboration, exploration, talking about it. How is the Christian "tradition" this particular tree which I have described? *In these ways*, one responds—and the metaphor is spelled out, and the tradition is given metaphorical form and meaning. Or the tradition of the Christian faith is a brick, made of clay, some mortar perhaps, some straw or other fiber, and then baked for hours and hours. *That* is what the Christian tradition is. How? It will require elaboration, but it will no doubt work, too, if the writer or speaker wishes it to work. *Anything* that the writer or speaker deems appropriate can be made into a metaphor: That is the metaphoric principle.

One Controlling Metaphor

When we turn our attention to the comic sermon, there are two major elements related to metaphor that we must take into account. The first is the place of metaphor in the comic sermon itself; the second is the matter of devising comic metaphors that will fit well within this particular sermon or that one.

First, then, what is the place of metaphor in the comic sermon? Let me go about it this way. Every sermon, like every speech, every novel or short story, every book, every poem, every formal act of communication, is built around a central motivating notion. The writer or speaker has something in mind to say and sets out to get it said, wherever that something originated.

It is for that one central idea, that motivating core of a literary work or of the sermon, that the comic metaphor does its best work. In other words, just as the sermon has one central idea, it also can have, if the sermon is to work most effectively, *one central metaphor*—a metaphor for that central idea. Every comic sermon, that is, has a controlling metaphor, one which embodies the central notion that the sermon seeks to convey or elicit. The sermon may have other, smaller metaphors, but each of them should in some way be related to or expand upon the central metaphor. This is what prevents the confusing pitfall of mixing one's metaphors in a sermon. It is true that too many different metaphors in a sermon create confusion and a sense of overload and breakdown. One metaphor is needed to shape the sermon's central thrust, whatever it is.

If one looks at Craddock's sermon again, "When the Roll Is Called Down Here," this principle, too, is effectively demonstrated. When one asks, in retrospect, What does that sermon set out to say, the answer may come back in different words from different people, but the "idea" gets through: "Treasure the people around you, particularly the ones in your journey who, one by one, lifted you to where you are today." However the preacher originally wrote that down, it is clearly the summary statement that he drew from the list of the Romans 16 text. But that idea is couched in a simple, remarkable metaphor: the comic metaphor of the "list." Oh, those lists. But in this sermon, even the metaphor has a wonderfully comic twist: The list is not a list; don't call it a list. Every piece of the sermon is about a list, a list that is not a list. These are real people; this is not a list. The list of jurors, real people. The list of the Romans 16 text, real people, not just a list. The list of those who "signed" the quilt. Real people—not just a list. The list on the Vietnam wall. The list that emerged and was given form at the Watts Bar Lake baptism. One metaphor undergirds the sermon, tying every piece together, with each piece reinforcing the others. The power and vividness of the sermon is in the controlling metaphor; it is the metaphor that makes the "point" of the sermon so easy to grasp and keep.

We need, though, to turn to our second major concern, and that is the problem of finding and creating metaphors that can serve as controlling agents in our sermons, metaphors like the non-list. The New Testament, of course, is filled with metaphors, from salt, light, juice and bread to vines and branches to white-washed tombs and mustard seeds. Metaphors are everywhere, all of them familiar items used to call into being some new or mysterious dimension of life. At the time they were first used, most of the metaphors of the New Testament were probably fresh and vibrant, incongruent, surprising. You are salt? What? What kind of idea is that? Salt is not a metaphor; it is a seasoning—until the speaker decides to make a metaphor out of it. Unexpected, and, when he said it, it probably packed a wallop of curiosity and memorability. Salt means what? Well, let's see, what do we know about salt? And how far can we push this if we are going to use salt to describe who and what we Christians are supposed to be? Our faith is like—a mustard seed? The mustard seed as metaphor. We know about mustard seeds, but what does knowing about them have to do with our faith? What an idea! Whoever eats my flesh and drinks my blood. Did he really say that? He didn't really say that, did he? Of course, it is metaphor, but some metaphors work and others don't. Who came up with this metaphor? Aren't we a little out of bounds here? And so on. Lighting a candle and then hiding it. You wouldn't light a candle on a dark evening and put a bushel basket over it, would you? It would immediately go out, right? So what good would the candle be? What if we poke some holes in the basket before we put it over the candle? That might not give much light to the room, but it would make a wonderful design on the walls and ceiling; and the candle probably wouldn't go out if the drafts in the room weren't too bad. We have to explore metaphors, to poke around in them, for them to come to life.

While we can still poke around, learn a few things, and even have some fun with the biblical metaphors, most of them by now have lost their originality, their punch, their energy. They are too familiar, as many have pointed out in recent years. It is true. Most of them are worn out. If the metaphor has lost its savor, where-with shall it do its metaphorical job, or something like that. The truth is that the Christian faith is badly in need of new metaphors—metaphors that arise from the world in which *we* live, metaphors that can again be original and fun, surprising, incongruous, comic, as well as true to the conceptualizations and ideas they are designed to bring to new life. *And this is where the comic vision and sensibility can come into play in a striking new form for the pulpit.*

The preacher becomes the maker of new metaphor; indeed, if the preacher does not do it, no one will; and it must be done. It requires not only a sense of delight, but daring. It requires a desire to explore and take risks, both in the study as one prepares and in the pulpit as one actually preaches the sermon. It requires a consciously keen eye and mind to take in virtually everything that one encounters as one goes through the day, whether in public or in the home. Again, one searching for new metaphor must remember that anything—anything!—has the potential of being turned into a metaphor for some aspect of Christian faith and life, and for the pulpit. Moreover, new metaphors are virtually always *jarring*, which, of course, is why they are usually comic in nature. New metaphors, in other words, often sound odd or out of place, since one will not have heard of "such a thing" before. But it is precisely in that oddity, that jarring incongruency, which the new metaphor carries that gives it its potency. The only question is whether the metaphor actually does "sum up" the meaning that its user (or creator) desires for it to have.

Connecting Metaphor and Idea

When the process is brought to the sermon, it begins with the preacher starting with the particular idea of what he or she wants to say; often it will be drawn from the study of a text, but sometimes not. My sermon is about this, and here is what I want to be able to say in the sermon. It is best when one makes such a thought conscious, rather than leaving it, as it otherwise will be, unconscious. The idea, then, is to create some metaphor, a controlling metaphor for the sermon, one that connects that central idea of the sermon with the congregants who must take that idea away with them, being able not only to have understood and digested it, but able also to experience it collectively or utilize it in some way in the living of life. So, in the preacher's mind during the mulling and the preparing is not only the idea about which one wants to speak, but also the question: What is this notion like? In other words: To say what I want to say is like saying…what? To put this into practice is like doing…what? It is like…what? This is the question that one turns over and over, looking, thinking, searching for that "what"; and that "what," when it is found, will be the sermon's metaphor. To find this metaphor, one does not look abstractly. Instead, one goes about the tasks and processes of living all the time looking, listening, staying open; doing other things, normal things, of course, but still looking for the "what." Coming up with an original metaphor is not an easy process. But it is a profoundly creative process, and if the preacher permits it to be, it is an extraordinarily comic process—which means it can also be quite unforgettable.

It is as it was for those who constructed the theologies and metaphors of the New Testament. What is faith like? We want to describe it and open up its multiple dimensions, and we want to do so in both an intellectual and experiential way. So faith is like…what? It is like, let us say, a mustard seed. A what? A mustard seed. Meaning what? It is small, tiny, or at least it can be. It is like someone who does not have much of it. My faith is small like …the smallness of the mustard seed. The mind is looking, thinking. But the mustard seed grows into a very large plant, leafy, giving shade, giving who knows what. From such a tiny bit, look what can grow. Yes, we can preach that. It is a strong, workable— but very odd and funny—metaphor. We want to explain the kingdom of heaven, so what is it like? It is like—and then the metaphors begin, simple metaphors that are often expanded into simple, straightforward stories and explanations. It is like this, and this, and this.

Say I am working on a sermon on the subject of evil. I have a text from a gospel or from Revelation. I have exegeted my text, and I am devising a particular way in which I want to look at evil, evil that is pervasive, elusive, and very difficult to deal with. Let me say—since I will draw from my own experience in the pulpit—that I am using Revelation chapter 13, since I am preaching a series of sermons through the Apocalypse of John. In chapter 13, evil is the explicit subject, and it is a big thing, with words like "behemoth" and "leviathan" used to talk about it, to symbolize it. For the people of Revelation, the Roman empire was most likely the evil the writer had in mind, and it was probably not lost on anyone who heard the words read. But I am stumped by the fact that these great beasts of Revelation do not work very well as metaphors for me, for our time, for my sermon. Roman empires don't translate very well. Such great beasts as these seem gone. Even the great Communist beast of my childhood has died and been buried. But I want to talk about evil, and I am fairly committed to this text. My brooding process begins, and I am brooding over the possibility of a new metaphor for evil, one that can connect to the text but that can spring me loose into something more up-to-date.

As happened in my case, as someone who lived at that time in the country, I came into the house late at night after being gone all day, turned on a light only to see a mouse make a quick getaway across the kitchen floor, disappearing under a cabinet. It was winter, and I had sensed that there were mice around, but I had never seen one like I did that time. I got on my hands and knees to search for him (him?), and in that position the idea of metaphor struck me. His tracks, his droppings, seemed everywhere once I started looking. I really became aware that the mouse I had seen had a lot of friends hiding around here somewhere. Here was, shall I say, evil in living form, in the form of a real beast; or at least that's how I felt. I don't want to be overly dramatic, but I had my Revelation 13 metaphor. The beasts of our time are not Big Beasts like behemoths and leviathans, but they are the Little Beasts. They are not the beasts that walk up to your front door demanding to be let in or they will break the door down—not those kind—but our beasts are the little beasts who sneak around in the dark, leaving their dirty tracks everywhere, and then fleeing quickly whenever someone turns on a light. The next day I let the two outdoor cats become indoor residents as well. They became part of my metaphorical package. The sermon that emerged from this experience and this metaphor is included in the Appendix of this book.

At another time, I was working on a sermon on the unity section of Ephesians 4, the text in which the extraordinary Greek words are compounded over and over again in order to emphasize both the nature and the intensity of unity in the church's family. I knew what I wanted to say: that the unity among us in the church is to be such that it *cannot* be pulled apart. I wanted a metaphor, one that would stick in the mind and heart. Early in the week, I was visiting an elderly church member who, while we chatted, was knitting. What she was doing caught my eye, even though I knew nothing whatsoever about such things as needlework or knitting. What I realized as we talked was that she was creating something complex out of a single piece of yarn; it just kept coming off of the large ball as she, without thinking, knitted away. My mind went to my sermon. I asked some questions about what she was doing and how she did it—some who are reading this will marvel at my ignorance. I asked her if she had something that she had knitted that I could have and explained to her the plan my mind was concocting. I had my metaphor, except this time I was going to treat it as visually and as dramatically as I could. It would be a comic metaphor in its unexpected sense.

When I preached in that church, I always stood between the pulpit and lectern on the open platform, speaking without notes. After going through the opening sections of my sermon, I began to speak about what this remarkable unity of Ephesians was, what it was like. As I did, I reached into the nearby pulpit for a pair of scissors and the large round doily that my friend had given me. I stretched it, held it up and marveled at its utter beauty and complexity, and then with a snip of the scissors, to the audible gasps of several in the congregation, I clipped one corner of it and began to pull on the yarn. What I unraveled was a single piece of yarn that went on and on and on, and I walked down the aisle, asking various ones to take hold of it. It is that kind of unity—*even taken apart, it is connected; even pulled apart so that its intricate beauty is unraveled, the yarn is never broken.* I liked that metaphor. Others have probably used it in different ways before me, but for me and my congregation it was new; and for those who shared it with joy and laughter that day, it was a wonderfully comic unfolding of a biblical idea.

Risky, Funny Metaphors

Some metaphors that one might devise are more bizarre, riskier. Sometimes the riskier they are, the funnier they are, and even the more memorable they are—and, contrary to some homiletical opinion, people tend to remember not just the metaphor, but usually what the metaphor was designed to call to mind and understanding, at least if it was fully explored as a metaphor and not just thrown out in passing. I once struggled with a text that set faith and love in tandem, as though the Christian experience involves both in some kind of balance, in tandem or tension, instead of one assuming a place as more important than the other— not an easy idea at all to explain. I went hunting for a controlling metaphor that might help me. I was sitting in a little diner on the

Friday before I was to preach—still with no metaphor—eating a bowl of clam chowder for lunch. My thoughts focused on my soup: Without the clams I have nothing but a bowl of what, of gruel of some sort—not bad tasting, but still gruel. I would not be inclined to eat such a thing. But, without the gruel, I would have nothing but a bowl of—clams; and, while some might like that, I certainly would not be able to eat them that way; I didn't like clams that well. What I realized, and it was a new thought to me, is that there is no such thing as clam chowder, which I like very much, without the chowder and the clams coming together in the same recipe. It is not a question of which is more important to the bowl of soup I enjoy; both are crucial, and if one is missing there is nothing, to my mind, worth eating. My clam chowder became my metaphor for the love and faith in balance sermon. Risky? Sure. Odd? Yes. Did it work? Yes, I think so. Is it a comic flavor for the sermon? It is certainly that.

Earlier I suggested that *anything* can be a potential metaphor for some idea or thought on which the sermon will be built. Any object, in other words, whatever it is, can be given meaning that it does not, of itself, possess; and the preacher, in the act of preaching, literally *creates* new meaning for whatever that object is. There has to be some reason why the preacher selects this particular object, and no other, to carry this new metaphorical meaning. Mice are, well, beasts; and in my sermon I invest a meaning into their "beastness" that gives them "new meaning," shall we say. In that same sermon, I also let a cat—since I know cats, too—become the "spirit of God" that is able to more than handle the beasts that are symbolized by my mice. That doily made of yarn is constructed in such a way that I can choose for it to "stand for" and even explain the unity that I find in the Ephesians text. I did not choose the doily randomly, or try to give it a metaphorical meaning which was incidental to it; its meaning, for me, was intricately connected to what the object itself was and how it was made. And the clam chowder? Well, it is a stretch, I know; and yet what I found in its actual properties lent itself to my investing those properties with meanings beyond what they actually were. Can one always devise or discover an original metaphor, a new metaphor, for every sermon? Perhaps not, and yet every sermon, in my judgment, is worth the effort. New metaphors are not only insightful, or capable of creating new insight, but they are also invariably funny; and when they are, they result in sermons that sparkle with light and memorability.

There is another way, though, for approaching the issue of metaphor, one that opens up just as many comic possibilities as the search for a single new metaphor does. It is what I will call the *narrative metaphor*, distinguishing it from what we have discussed so far as the *object metaphor*. It, too, is a comic device that can find its way into the sermon. The narrative metaphor is a particular line of action or behavior; like the object metaphor it is a very common, everyday action that arises from the often-invisible processes of living life in its most mundane forms. The metaphorical process is basically the same as we have already described it. It begins with a sermon idea, with a sense of "here is what I want to say." It is followed, then, with a "but what is that like?" This time, though, instead of one searching for some "object" to serve as an explanatory metaphor, one searches for a particular situation or action. That is: It is like *doing*...this! Or, it is like *doing*...that! It is not the object as metaphor, but it is some *action* as metaphor; and just as the object usually needs to be described in some detail in order for it to be invested with metaphorical meaning, here the action itself can be described in detail—often in wonderfully comic detail—as a way of investing it with metaphorical meaning, as well. In my experience in sermon preparation, object metaphors are most valuable when used with concepts and ideas, while narrative, or action, metaphors are best used with ethical or behavioral notions or directives.

The key to narrative metaphor is recognition. The actions that are set up and described must be universal ones; they must be *fully recognizable* by everyone who hears them. *The comedy, in fact, is in that recognition*. The more the recognition, the more the comedic shines through. And when some bits of exaggeration are added to the narrative metaphor as it is told, the more intensely the comedy of the situation is experienced. The telling of the narrative, moreover, must embody what John Vorhaus, a well-known comedy writer, has called both "truth and pain." The narrative, that is, has to be truthfully or recognizably described; and the pain in those narrative situations must be, if not shared by all, at least understood by all.

For example, we have to go a lot of places and do a lot of things that we do not want to do; but there is no good way out of them. The consequences of not doing this or that—one can fill in the blank—are too serious not to go through with it. The whole thing is a lot like a trip to the dentist, although I hope dentists can forgive my characterization here. The narrative metaphor is established, and one will use its comic aspects to talk about something very serious. But the metaphor must now be developed—in all its "truth and pain." The truth is that we have to go to the dentist, as much as we may not want to do so; and the pain is that unpleasant things (many of us still believe) happen at the dentist's office—dentists do know this, don't they? The experience can be spelled out in as much vivid (and comic) detail as possible in the time one has to tell it.

I do not want to go to the dentist. I do not like to go to the dentist. It is about childhood teeth trauma or something like that. I will try everything I can think of to not have to go to the dentist. Maybe I will be sick when it is time to go; no, better, maybe the dentist will be sick. I will stay home to wait for the telephone call telling me that the dentist has canceled my appointment. No, it looks like it is on, and I have to go. Maybe when I get there and get into that awful chair I will just keep my mouth shut. No, that will not work. OK, open your mouth—wider, wider, wider, wider, wider, wider, wider, wider. That did it. I opened my mouth so wide I turned inside out. It won't open any wider. This won't hurt a bit. Right! Keep your eyes closed tightly so you can't see the size of this two-fisted needle. It's an electric cattle prod in my mouth. My entire backside just went numb. The sound of that drill. Middle East oil is pulled up from the ground with smaller drills than these. The description can go as far with as much imagination and exaggeration as the good storyteller can give it. The trip to the dentist can become a *narrative metaphor* for some larger, ultimate experience of life. The preacher makes the connection.

One's imagination is called to its fullest work here, but when this process is done well, it is a rich, shared comic experience—a common human experience that has, or can have, meaning far beyond the narrative itself. Something else can be "like standing in a long line, say, waiting to see a movie, and the kid in front of you is making faces at you in the line." So what do you do with such an annoyance? The telling can go through an exaggerated series of ways of trying to cope with such a simple happening. First, you try to ignore the kid—one would describe how that works. When that fails, one tries to get the attention of the adult with the kid, an adult who is reading a magazine and paying no attention whatsoever. One tries to get the adult's attention, at least at first, in a civilized fashion, with some clearings of the throat, perhaps. When that doesn't work, one tries to maintain one's dignity while deciding to outdo the kid by making faces at him. All the while, the situation is deteriorating. There is truth to be told here; and there is also much pain involved in the telling. But everyone recognizes the situation; everyone also empathizes, and everyone gets a sense of how metaphorically this simple narrative speaks of much larger problems of coping well, or not coping well, with life.

Or, something may be "like hunting for a small jar of pimento in an enormous grocery store that one has never visited before." How does one go about that? Its truth is that one must find the jar of pimento, and the pain is that there is no one around to help, and one is hunting for the proverbial needle in the haystack. How does one keep one's cool and search for something that does not appear to fall under any of those signs that hang with large numbers above each of the thirty-five aisles in the store? That hunt, which can be great comedic fun in a sermon, can serve as the narrative metaphor for any number of things spiritual or ethical that a sermon might address.

Or, something else might be like "taking one's on-the-road driving test," another of those dreadful, if not near-universal experiences. I am aware that not everyone takes, or has taken, a driving test, so that I must be careful not to cast aspersions on those who, for whatever reason, do not drive. Yet the truth is that for the vast majority of people, from teenagers to senior citizens, taking the road test to get a driver's license is one of those potentially painful experiences in which if something can go wrong, it is just liable to do so. We forget and pull into the crosswalk before we stop for the stop sign; and as soon as we are there and realize what we have done, it is too late. The examiner silently begins making copious notes while we try to figure out what to do or say that might get us out of this one. Or we forget and turn the front wheels away from the curb instead of toward it. Or we get nervous and do some other dumb thing that under normal driving conditions we would never forget to do. It is one of those experiences from which narrative metaphor can be constructed and with good humor in it as well.

Or, trying something else: Narrative metaphor might be baking a fancy cake for really special company due in less than an hour, only to realize that the recipe card has omitted the precise amounts of two crucial ingredients called for by the recipe. What to do now, and how will we try to get ourselves through this one and still get the cake made; and if we guess wrong about those two ingredients, what will we say about a cake that doesn't quite, shall we say, make it? The point that such a narrative metaphor might make? You fail, you knew you were going to fail, it is an embarrassing kind of failure, more like a faux pas; but you always try to cover up for yourself. And what lengths we will go to to cover up something so as not to be embarrassed.

In all such cases, we start with a predicament and create a story from it. We think imaginatively. We make it up, using exaggeration, following a plausable story premise, but stretching it to absurd lengths or dimensions. In doing so, we create comic narrative metaphors. *This* type of behavior is like *that* type of behavior. From idea to metaphor. Metaphors are complex, no question about that. But comic sermons cannot exist without them. Preachers take risks when they create new metaphors, no doubt about that either. Still, sermons never fail to come alive under the spell of new metaphor. And, granted all of our concerns about being true to Bible and gospel, we are deeply in need today of those sermons about which one can say that they came alive.

7

The Comic Bible:
Fusing Imagination and Text

It is, by now, nothing new to point out that the Bible, both in its Old and New Testaments, contains many comic elements and possibilities. Stretching from the laughter of Sarah in Genesis to the witticisms of the Proverbs to the hyperboles, puns, and parables of Jesus in the Gospels to what appear to be celebratory festivals imagined in the New Jerusalem of Revelation, the comic spirit is not missing from Holy Scripture. As scholars like Elton Trueblood and, more recently, Doug Adams have taught us, the preacher can indeed *find* the comic spirit rustling through the pages of biblical text, both Old and New; and those findings need to have a place, wherever and whenever possible, in our preaching.

In addition, however, to finding comic elements in scripture, it is also important for the preacher to know how to *create* comedic elements—based on biblical text—for the sermon. Two relatively new biblical awarenesses have opened up numerous doors for the working of the comic spirit in this active, imaginative, creative process vis-à-vis biblical writing.

The first is an awareness that what we have in the biblical documents, particularly in the New Testament, are very *short*, summary statements, recollections, or even creations of those who wrote the words down. Today's readers of popular novels (and they are legion) are used to pages upon pages of description, character development, scene setting, and dialogue, and within that context the biblical stories are ridiculously sparse, spare, incomplete—more charitably, we might say concise to the utmost. In the Gospels, the stories—even the overall "story" of Jesus—is wrapped up in a few short pages; individual stories are told in no more than a few paragraphs at most. We are so used to reading them just as they are that we easily overlook how much is actually left out. A few details, a short bit of teaching, a snippet of dialogue, and the story is over—if we get even that much. Where are the rest of the details? Where are the elaborations of idea and interaction? Why don't we hear more of what went on between people? As biblical scholars and some homileticians are now beginning to sense, we can ask dozens upon dozens of perfectly good questions about a biblical story—about what happened, and how it happened, and even why it happened; we can do that about literally every page of our gospel accounts.

This, itself, is a remarkable opening for the comic spirit to do its work in its encounter with biblical story. We can fill in details. We can use our imaginations—not to change things in our biblical stories, but to enjoy that play of filling in, even constructing or creating, dimensions that are actually missing from the Bible's stories and texts.

Changes in Our Understanding

The second important and relatively recent awareness (as strange as this may seem) that opens a new opportunity for the comic spirit in dealing with biblical text is that we can never really understand a written text from long ago and far away. No matter what kind of text it is, its meaning is seldom more than ambiguous at best, and often nothing short of enigmatic. We can learn some things about a particular text, of course, and saying all this is in no way to disparage the painstaking and important efforts of biblical scholars, past or present. We can sometimes even make fruitful inferences about what an author might have had in mind or what those who were contemporaries with the text might have found in it. The key word here, though, is "might." What we now know quite well is the sheer elusiveness of a text's meaning. A text, at best, can mean many things, depending on how one treats it or what one brings to it—and we all bring something unique to it, whoever we are. There is simply no way to authoritatively say, "This is what it means," or "I know for certain that this text means this." It cannot be done, and most biblical scholars and preachers are coming to terms with that.

For some homileticians, this new understanding means that the preacher must be extremely cautious about saying *anything* beyond the text itself save for those few pieces of background or implication that can safely be known or drawn about a text. However, since the text is fundamentally ambiguous as far as its background and meaning are concerned, *it is possible to turn the argument completely around.* That is, one assumes that if a text has a specific meaning, it will resolutely withhold it; so the best the preacher or interpreter can do is to *interact* with the text, talking to it and listening to it, dancing around it and asking, or urging, the text to join in the dancing, as it were. One decides to have fun with the text, assuming that, despite its sometime seriousness, the text would not mind the fun at all. From this perspective, it is not so much a detective at work in the text as it is a jester. One becomes free to use the full, rich resources of one's imagination in querying the text, first from this vantage point, then from that one, then from still another and another. One is not looking for the truth of the text; one simply wants to make the text one's companion, calling it from a kind of inertia to an *experience* full of life and joy and imaginative vibrance. And with this, of course, the creative, comic spirit kicks in and drags the text along.

One does all of this openly, in fact, in both the preparation and the preaching of the sermon. When one turns the comic spirit loose in the biblical text, the text itself invariably responds in some comic fashion. This means that for the preacher to imaginatively explore a biblical character's motivation in a sermon is *not* something "dangerous"—of course we cannot actually "know" the character's motivations, as some homileticians rightly warn us. But *because* they are not in the text, we are free to poke around, imaginatively, into what they *might* have been or what they *could* have been. In so doing, we are not asserting that we know this or know that; we are only deciding to make inquiry into them, comic inquiry into them, shall we say; and we will keep everything playful and open-ended and available for others to join in with our comic imaginings. It is not dangerous, either, for us to imaginatively wonder how a particular event, described very sparsely, *might* have happened. We do not know what happened or how it happened, of course; nor will we ever. But since we will never know, we are free to wonder, to imaginatively create: maybe this, maybe that, could have been this, could have been that. Who knows? Might have been, right?

To use one's imagination is to hypothesize, to see things from new and unexpected directions. It is to ask strange, irrelevant, even impertinent questions and then to pursue those questions wherever they might lead us. It is to shuffle the deck one more time. And then maybe do it again. We will play games, good games, "what if" games. We will wear our funny hats with their tassles and bells and our pointed shoes in the court of the holy, the clown doing silly, skittish things in front of the king. But they will still be serious things, despite their silliness; and neither the holiness nor the solemnity of the "court" will be damaged by what we silly types do. That is how the comic spirit interacts with sacred scripture. It simply refuses to let the sacredness of the scripture go to its head.

Once it is acknowledged that we can use our comic imaginations on biblical text, then it becomes a matter of how to do it. Four different forms of comic interaction with a text will be examined here, even though they are all interrelated and in some cases, despite their differences, they overlap. What is common to all of these forms is their overt dependence on comic imagination and "what if" ways of pushing and pulling on the text, of challenging the text, of hearing it and then talking back to it. Mind you, this is not all done merely as exegesis, or as exegetical *preparation* for preaching. This is done as a part of the sermon itself. The playfulness that begins in the study is replayed and continued in the pulpit, not in any way that might be deemed sacrilegious, but as a way to make the text vital and accessible, just as the jester does in prodding the royals into laughter at themselves. It is biblical play, serious play.

Juxtaposing Bible, Present

The first and the most rudimentary comedic form of interacting with the biblical text, the one that most preachers have tried at some time or other, is the process of juxtaposing the past and the present, the biblical world and the present world. It works comedically because of the incongruity principle that we discussed in an earlier chapter, the process of placing things together that do not go together. So one takes the Abraham of old with his extended family and places them in, say, Orange Country, California. Now we conjure up the Abraham story of one being called on to move, directed even by some unseen force from some place; but the move is not from the Ur of Chaldees to a place which "I will show you," but from Anaheim to someplace up north—a place which, at some point along the way, "I will show you." Not even Triple A knows where you are going. It is intriguing and potentially very funny to think about the Abraham story that way. It requires not only the best of one's imaginative abilities, but it also provokes some serious ethical and theological thinking as well—*if* we are going to take this kind of comic juxtaposition seriously. It is one thing to have God talking to Abraham back then about moving; it is quite another thing, a comic thing, to have God talking to the Abraham Moskowitz of Orange County. It is Bill Cosby's classic comedy routine of God trying to get Noah's attention.

The comic, and theological, possibilities of this, moreover, are virtually endless. Any biblical character moved into a contemporary setting prompts imaginative reworking. And no two preachers will ever work the juxtaposed situation in the same way or come to the same theological or ethical insights. No two preachers will ever initiate the same kind of laughter from such incongruity, either, which is part of the originality and the fun of such a comic undertaking. If one takes Matthew, for example, the tax collector, and makes him an IRS agent, where would we come out? One could have some serious fun with that. What do we generally think of IRS agents? Does that help us understand the attitude toward Matthew? Let's go through an audit—only those of us who have been audited can fully appreciate this—with Matthew the IRS agent. He is, shall we say, then called by God. Will he resign from the IRS? What changes will he make in his life, in his attitudes toward people? What will he carry into his "new life" from his old one? Have Matthew, now called by God, do an IRS audit! Will people ever forget that he was once a hard-bitten IRS investigator? One's imagination can easily fill in a host of other questions and other details—and do so with as much flair and comic intent as one wishes.

This is true with major characters like Noah or Joseph or Matthew or Peter or Paul, or even Jesus; but it is also true, and often more interesting, when the same thing is done with minor or even unnamed characters. A farmer, for instance, described in a parable by Jesus, might be juxtaposed into the modern world of farming. The question, then, would be how that farmer would perform, and even problem-solve, within the modern farmer's world. I grew up in farming communities of the Midwest; I detassled corn and cut weeds out of bean fields as a youth, so I am not unfamiliar with farming. In my preparation of a sermon doing this, though, I would probably take time to call one of my old friends back in the Midwest who actually took over the family farm and is struggling still to make a go of farming. I would fill in some background and some specifics that grow out of simple telephone research—and it will all become part of my new farming parable, my comic story about that character from Jesus' words.

One could also take a character like the rich young man in Mark 10 who asked Jesus what he needed to do to inherit eternal life. One could place that nameless character in the business community of today, wherever one might imagine it to be. More than that, one could also say that the young man goes to a preacher—who will, let's say, represent Jesus—and asks the same question of the preacher. Who is this young man when placed in that contemporary setting? What will he—or she, since it may be a woman just as easily—be like? From what background? With what assets? What will the preacher say? What are the preacher's concerns and interests when confronted with the question from this particular person in an expensive suit? One can create a fascinating conversation, working it in correlation—or in contrast—with the biblical story. Humor is generated and the story comes alive, if the preacher lets a playful imagination shape the way the story emerges. Theological and ethical insight will be the outcome as well.

This process also works the other way around, even though this orientation is seldom used in preaching. It is still a juxtapositional situation, however. It is one that places a person of today—say a farmer or a businessman or even a preacher—back into a biblical setting. In some ways, this approach has more potential than the first, since it requires more of the preacher and since it is so unexpected. For example, what if we take a young, well-to-do attorney (from Orange County, again?)—let's make him someone who is also fairly well known to the public—and put him in the place of the rich young man of the gospel story. Our attorney is not disinterested in spiritual things; so, fascinated with Jesus—Jesus also being a rising young professional in his own right (we're imagining)—the attorney decides to spend some time listening to this teacher. He gets caught up in the excitement of it all and pushes through the crowd and asks Jesus his question: "What do you and I have to do to team up? I am interested in what you have, and I think you should be interested in what I could do for you." Jesus is intrigued. He sizes him up: three-piece Armani suit, Italian silk tie, expensive Bruno whatever shoes, gold chains, Rolex on his arm—Jesus takes it all in. What is Jesus going to say? You can fill it in, but do so in the context of the man to whom Jesus is speaking. Play with it. Have fun with it. It is two cultures, then and now, in imaginative juxtaposition, incongruently set together. Work it through. Ask the "what ifs," not as exegesis, but as the sermon itself. Create their conversation and let the sermon reflect what should be probing, haunting—and comic—interplay. Its "play" will be both poignant and funny. Let the incongruities be felt, even though the ideas arise from the first century and are going to have to be assimilated by a wealthy lawyer from the twenty-first. Such juxtapositions are make-believe, to be sure. They are imaginary. But they work as comic ways of thinking about old questions and issues in new forms.

Seeing Texts Naively

The second way in which one can interact with biblical text in a comic fashion is in looking at texts—at most, though not necessarily all, texts—in what the linguistic philosopher Paul Ricoeur called a naive way. From the comic perspective, it is the idea of looking at a text the way a child would do so, asking simple (not simplistic), naive questions. The questions, though, are designed not so much to elicit answers as to call attention to the process of inquiry itself. It is not unlike the comic story of the hundreds of people watching the king parade down the street naked, but since it is the king everyone applauds politely, afraid to speak of what they see. It takes a child to look up at her mother and ask why the king has no clothes on. It is a simple—naive—question that does not appreciate the gravity of the deception, a deception that may have happened so often that no one ever thinks twice about it. The preacher, not only in sermon preparation but also in sermon presentation as well, *becomes that child*, asking the naive questions, the obvious questions.

This is, in a sense, a kind of *language* humor, the kind that George Carlin is famous for. Why does one say that? Why is that word used there? What does that word mean? Doesn't it really sound funny saying it that way? For example, in Matthew 3 we are introduced to John the Baptist, the one who came "preaching in the desert." The NIV then says at verse 4: "John's clothes were made of camel's hair, and he had a leather belt around his waist. His food was locusts and wild honey." Wait. Stop there. Let's go through that once again. Clothes of camel's hair. So what would he look like? What does he have on? He came from where? From the desert? If we really try to get to the bottom of this, where did he live? He's homeless, right? Cave dweller? Is this by choice, or is this guy as eccentric as this is starting to sound? Wait a minute. Let's get back to the clothes, even though where he has been living and these clothes he is wearing may have something to do with each other? Homeless guy, dressed in camel's hide. If one is homeless, where exactly does one get such camel's hide?—or do I even want to think about this? And he eats what? Let's think about this. He eats locusts. Locusts? How? Let's see if we can imagine how this works. They make all of that screeching noise in the early evening, don't they? So he had to spend some time every evening gathering his dinner. They're easy to hear, but never easy to actually find, as I recall from hearing them back in Illinois. How many locusts would it take to make a good meal, would you think? Well, I think I've got a dozen or so here in my sack; that should about do me for tonight. If somebody stopped to have dinner with John out there some night, wherever he lived, he would have to tell them that they were having locusts, wouldn't he? Not likely he had very many guests, wouldn't you say? But he also was big on wild honey, the text says. Bee hives—there are wild bee hives out there, and John not only knows where they are, but you have to be impressed: He knows how to get that honey out of the wild bee hives without being stung to kingdom come, if you will pardon the expression.

In some ways, a comically naive reading is one that tries to see a text by always, under every circumstance, taking its language *literally*, at its face value. It is not a skeptical viewpoint, really; it is, instead, a "simple" viewpoint that wants very much to keep in touch with the real world of "how things are." It wants to subject everything to some kind of "reality" test, even though that test is quite of the reader's own making. In all this it focuses initially and primarily on language, on the specific words that are written down. Why does it say that? Why is that word used here and that one there? I think I know what that word means, but what *could* it mean here, and why does it mean that? I know that the sentence says that, but does it really mean "that"? Or, if it really means that, how could that possibly be? Or, if that could possibly *be*, then how did it actually happen? Or, if it happened that way this time, why didn't it do so the last time? And so on. The naive questions of a child, the curiosities of someone incurably curious. Not a doubter, but the probings of someone who is encountering something for the first time and who comes up short in understanding it all. Why is that? Why? When? Who says? It is like every word, every term, is a shiny rock that must be held up to the light so that it can be examined and marveled over before it is put back down with the other shiny rocks.

This is a playing out of the naive question-asking process. It is, or at least it can be, inherently comic. In addition, it is also a fairly harmless way to demystify certain texts, to let people hear old texts read and explored in entirely new ways; not so much by giving the text a new or different interpretation, but by letting the text break *itself* open in imaginative and often unexpected ways. One can ask the questions, can press question upon question, in effect, listening with an "Oh yeah?" kind of response, and letting the text stand up to a kind of comic scrutiny, which it virtually always will. To read a text naively, asking questions about the literality of its language, is a simple way to distance ourselves from the text. It is in that distancing that we are able to interact with it, not giving the text full control, but not trying to control it, either. We simply engage the text in a playful, but deeply useful, repartee. Here is where discovery takes place. In this naive process of discovery, there is both incongruity and surprise. We are able to learn and to laugh at the same time.

Filling in Missing Pieces

The third form of comedy that can arise from the interaction with biblical text is the one that results from the preacher's imaginative construction of *missing* situations and details in biblical story, character, and even admonition, something to which we referred earlier in this chapter. There, we spoke about the economy of biblical language; so much is said in such a small space. Stories are sketched with a few verbal brush strokes, characters are painted, often with great power, in a few well-selected details, and teachings are sketched aphoristically yet with remarkable precision. It is as though someone decided to leave it to others to connect the dots, to finish coloring the page, to fill in the blank spaces. And there are plenty of them to fill in. So one of the great comic processes in one's dealing with scripture is in imaginatively "finishing" the story. In many religious traditions, in the Protestant African American tradition for example, this has been a staple of preaching for many years.

If one takes a simple, well-known story like the presentation of the infant Jesus in the temple for his circumcision before Simeon, it is told in Luke 2 in a concise, straightforward narrative. If one wishes to preach it, or from it, one wants the story to come alive. To make it spring, as it were, into vividness, one must give it a range of detail and color that can only arise from the preacher's imagination, indeed, from the preacher's *comic* imagination.

Let's go back to the Lukan story of Jesus' presentation. It begins: "When the time of their purification according to the law of Moses had been completed, Joseph and Mary took him (Jesus) to Jerusalem to present him to the Lord" (Luke 2:22, NIV). How simple and direct. But to bring this to full, wondrous life, one must imaginatively create "the" story behind the simple line. This is a big-time event in the life of a young couple. It seems easy enough, matter-of-fact enough, and yet it is probably big-time nervous time. Is there shopping to do to get everything ready? Where do the clothes for the event come from? One can see that this process of story-creation is not unlike the asking of naive questions. But here the difference is that we are going to create the story—*a story*—behind the line of the biblical text. The baby is only a few days old, acting, one must assume, like any baby a few days old would act. What happens the day of the presentation? One might want to sketch the day, using the best "real" information of that era one can come up with. But beyond that, we will be clear about our "wonderings" and our imaginative creating. Who goes to the temple with them? Honestly, we do not know, so the storyteller receives considerable freedom to create the answer to the question. Then, as verse 24 says, they have to offer a sacrifice when they get there: "a pair of turtledoves or two young pigeons". Is this Joseph's responsibility? Maybe a little research will indicate where the birds are to come from, but Joseph has to be concerned about this. What goes through his mind on the way to the

temple? Will he have to pay a visit to the court of the money changers and the merchants who, no doubt, have many birds for sale,
the money changers that Jesus, as a young adult, would also visit?
Does he leave Mary and the baby in the courtyard while he goes
to purchase the sacrificial birds? One imagines a story. One
sketches details, not real details but make-believe details; and one
says so. The text will be followed, of course; in fact, the text will
guide. But the text will only become the scaffolding for a wonderfully comic story, one that will be filled with color and recognizable life.

Other lines of the infant presentation story may be imagined,
too. There is old Simeon. We know something about Simeon, as
he is sketched in the text. Simeon had been told that he would not
die, the text says, until he had seen the "consolation of Israel."
And now he senses—how?—that the babe being brought in for
consecration is that child. The text says only that he was "moved
by the spirit," and in that moving, as it were, he seems to have
known. But let's get closer to Simeon if we are going to tell a story,
if we are going to bring this story fully to life. Simeon is in his
study, working on the commentary on Job that he has been writing for fifty-odd years. The door opens. An aide hollers, "They're
here." And he was thinking such a fine thought at the moment,
too. He sets the papers aside and slowly gets up. As he rises, new
thoughts begin to stir—no Alzheimer's here. Maybe it's just a
vague sense of something. One might describe what goes on in
Simeon's head—describe this "something" that the text calls being "moved by the spirit." What a good story could be spun from
it. True to the text. But bringing the text joyously alive. Humanizing the words of a text that are otherwise just words, words that
have been read too long and too often. Can these words still live?
Yes, they can, but only by the storyteller's imaginatively comic art.

Simeon concludes his short speech, one that is probably off-
the-cuff for the first time in decades for him. New words, concluding with: "And a sword will pierce your own soul too" (Luke
2:35b, NIV). What? What did he just say? Joseph turns to Mary
quizzically, a look that quickly has a tinge of anger. Mary looks at
Joseph. She looks down at the child, and then at the floor. Joseph
is tense. What did that mean? A sword? Where is the happiness,
the blessing of long life and good health? Wait a minute. Fortu-
nately, that old prophetess Anna was there, too. The text says that
she came up to Mary and Joseph "at that very moment." It's a

good thing. Somebody had to break the tension. She had seen it and heard it, and she was still very sharp, despite her age, probably a lot sharper about things like that than old Simeon. She quickly came up to offer a prayer and say (the text tells us) all of the good things that old Simeon didn't get around to. It is a wonderfully human story, a comic story in many ways, but a comic story only if one is willing to create the comedy of the story's details.

The two other forms of this process are also fairly well known, but use of them requires more care and practice than most preachers have given to them. One is character study. Characters of both Old and New Testaments, even major characters, are sketched at best, and then sketched only in their "objective" behavioral modes. Even a character like Joseph, whose life occupies something like half of the book of Genesis, is told as an exterior story. Like the story of Simeon and Anna in the temple, it is a story that one must bring to life, and one does that by taking pieces of the story—often a small bit—and filling it in, retelling it with creative, human imaginings. A New Testament character like Peter or John, or a lesser character like Timothy or Philemon, characters that have been told and retold for centuries, still must be rethought, reimagined and reconfigured. The comic mind must probe into their minds, following whatever clues might be available from the text, but then supplying the very best of what one knows or conjures up from human experience.

The other form of this comic storytelling from biblical text might be described as situational. This is an approach that can be utilized when dealing with *didactic* or *theological* texts, with epistle texts, for example. Invariably, the preacher will begin sermon preparation on such a text with some fundamental exegetical work, that is, learning as much as possible about the circumstances of both the writing and the receiving of the epistle in which the text is located. Most often, some basic facts are found in a commentary, sometimes agreed upon, sometimes controversial. Whatever one finds, however, can serve as a kind of "behind the scenes text" for the written text, but from that point on, the preacher's imagination can fill in a background for the text, whether for its writing or reception. The process of doing this can be seen, again, in Prof. Craddock's sermon "When the Roll Is Called Down Here." One wants to connect that imagined background to the text as much as possible, of course, in order not to be accused of just making up anything for a good story. But a good story is still what one wants to come up with here. And it should be a story filled with color and life, with bustle and intrigue and motive. It may have its own cast of imaginary characters who prompt the text's writing, or characters who are going to receive the text when it is sent, and who are probably going to have to figure out what to do with the text when they get it. One can only imagine (as one should) what kind of board meeting took place once one of those letters from Paul arrived for reading to the congregation. But what fun one can have with such imaginings; and what insightful thinking might actually result from such comic probings.

From Present to Past

There is a fourth general form of comic interaction with biblical text, one similar in some ways to these others we have discussed, but one that is also strikingly different as well. It involves the process of exploring things in the present, and then *inferring those things back into the text's own stories and teachings.* Let me illustrate what I mean like this. I have long been fascinated with the relationship between Jesus and his cousin John, John the Baptist. The details of it in the gospels are sketchy, at best, but just enough is told to create all sorts of intriguing wonderings. They were six months apart, John six months older. We get the story of John coming preaching in the wilderness or the desert, the country boy; in the middle of the story Jesus arrives, requesting baptism. John sees Jesus coming and it interrupts everything he is doing. They converse, warmly and respectfully, and John baptizes his cousin. They go separate ways, but they seem close. They keep track of each other. John sends questions to Jesus, important questions. Jesus receives word of John's martyrdom. None greater than John has ever lived, Jesus tells those around him. It is a remarkable story that reveals a thoroughly remarkable relationship.

But so much is left out. We find ourselves wondering what was going on between them. What *had* gone on between them? How did they affect each other? How did they feel about each other? Here is what I want to do comically, imaginatively. I think I can fill in something of their relationship because I grew up in Illinois with a first cousin with whom I was very close from a very young age. He, too, was older than I, by about a year. He grew up in and lived in the country, the rural area of what we capitalized as Southern Illinois. I was a city boy; we lived in central

Illinois in a "city" of fewer than a thousand people. Every summer from my earliest memory until mid-high school, I would go to Southern Illinois to stay from two weeks to a month with my country cousin Charles. Those were the glory weeks of my growing up. We were cousins, as close as any two individuals could ever be. I was closer to Charles than I ever was during those years to my brother John, who was two years younger than I. At the same time, though, there was distance between me and Charles. We were from different places, but not just geographically. We were distinct from each other, and we knew it. In fact, we valued it. We taught each other things from our very different "worlds." Charles taught me how to chase water moccasins, those deadly swamp snakes that are so plentiful in rural Southern Illinois. It required a good piece of thin, four-foot-square plywood and a long forked stick. The stick was for stirring up the snake nests to enjoy watching them slither and scatter, and the plywood was to make sure that none of them could get to us when they came our direction. We camped out at night. I ate things I would never have eaten, except that Charles "taught" me how. I taught him about slingshots and homemade guns that shot knotted sections of innertube—city-boy types of activities. I taught him about soap box derby racing cars, and about building things. And we talked. Day and night we talked and dreamed. We talked about girls—about specific girls, ones that he knew down south and ones that I knew up north. We talked about our fears, our parents, our conquests, which became much more in the talking that they ever were in the doing. We talked about what life was going to be like, about who and what we wanted to be. We lay under the stars and laughed. When tragedy hit our family, which it did, we lay under the stars and cried together. I remember those wonderful cousin days with Charles. Of course we have kept in touch. Sort of. But when we see each other, we talk about our families, our kids, for awhile; but *then* we talk about what it was like back then chasing snakes and making slingshots.

I think I understand a lot about Jesus and John. I think I can fill it a lot of details, imaginary details, of course; and yet boy cousins—maybe girl cousins, too, I don't know about that—are probably a lot alike no matter where they grow up. I think Jesus went every summer out to the desert for a couple of weeks with John. I think John showed him every cave and every high, secret boulder he knew so well. I think Jesus and John chased snakes and ate locusts together. I think John taught Jesus how to get honey out of a wild beehive without getting stung. I think they lay under the stars and talked and dreamed, talked about girls and dreamed of what they would do someday. I think that John and Jesus hadn't seen each other in quite a while until that day that John, like Charles a very religious country boy, saw Jesus coming over the hill. And all of those long wonderful days and nights of childhood came rushing back. I am making all of this up, of course; I am just playing the jester. But I know cousins. I know the pain that Jesus felt when he heard that his cousin John had been killed by that old Herod. And I know the tears that probably filled his eyes when he told everyone around him that no one better had ever walked the earth than his cousin John. He meant that. It wasn't just a tribute. He meant that. We can tell stories like that, wonderfully comic stories. The possibilities of such stories—stories of the past inferred from stories in the present—are everywhere between here and biblical lore, between here and the Old Testament, or the New. They are imaginative, made-up; and yet they are not made-up at all. They are very real. That is what gives them their comic intensity.

All of the pieces that we have sketched in this chapter are interrelated. They can be practiced and used, not as discrete ways of interacting with biblical story and text, but as ways from which those interactions can be comically combined and fleshed out. And it all should be fun. The biblical texts on which one draws should be fun to play with. So many good homileticians have worked on the subject in recent years that we, as preachers, are finally starting to really grasp the power of the human imagination in our sermons. But it is not imagination as opposed to the text. It is the imagination, the comic imagination, fully aligned with the text, fused with the text, as a profound form of comic biblical conjuring.

8

The Comic Persona:
Being Somebody in the Pulpit

The comic spirit possesses one other important, though subtle and often overlooked, ingredient, one that, like the others, can readily find its way into the pulpit. It is the ability of the preacher to laugh at himself or herself in the course of the sermon. It requires the development of what is sometimes called one's own comic persona. This means that the preacher, in a gentle and dignified way, chooses to play the role of the clown; not to "clown" or cut up in any way, but to do in the sermon what the clown does in the circus or rodeo: that is, to break tension or to keep the intensity of very serious things from becoming overwhelming. It is, as Garrison Keillor put it, to keep our "faith cheerful" and our sense of God and ourselves seasoned with "gentleness and humor." When this aspect of the comedic spirit is understood and practiced well, it is one of the most delightful and charismatic of the tools that can grace the pulpit.

We have to be very careful here, though, since of all the elements in the comic process this one is usually the most problematic for homileticians and preachers. The problem is that, for some generations now, preachers have been sternly taught that they

127

are never to intrude themselves into their sermons. No mention of self, no calling attention to self, as it is usually put, can be allowed, since that interferes with or detracts from the presentation of the gospel. This viewpoint, though, is part and parcel with the idea that one should never tell one's own stories from the pulpit; that those personal stories, the "I" stories, also deflect attention from the gospel to the preacher, who is supposed to remain neutral, if not invisible. The preacher, in this view, is only the carrier of the message, the hand or the voice; and the preacher's personality or persona is never to interfere with the message that is being delivered. What we know in and for our time, however, and what we examined in an earlier chapter, is that the gospel, if it is to be the gospel, must *pass through* the life and experience of the preacher. In fact, it cannot *not* pass through the preacher, at least not without becoming very sterile and distant. There is no such thing as preacher neutrality; or, if there is, what results from it is a kind of sterility, a sterility that once might have been accepted as the norm, but that in our day is experienced by a congregation as empty, hollow. Today, people who come to church are deeply concerned about who the preacher is, and about the preacher's relationship to what is being said in the pulpit. Today, they want to know if the preacher is genuine, a real "flesh and blood" person and not a "stuffed shirt." Today, they want to know what the preacher experiences, whether the preacher ever cries or feels depressed or…laughs.

So it is not surprising that the preacher's own stories, judiciously told, are welcomed today as a sign of authenticity and credibility. What goes along with that, however, is the very high value that is also placed on the ability of the preacher to engage in *playful self-deprecation*, the willingness of the preacher to laugh *at* himself or herself. It is more than that, though. It is the value placed by the hearers of our sermons on our demonstrating that, in biblical language, we do not think of ourselves more highly than we ought to think. While there are many ways, of course, to do this, one of the most accessible and comedic is the development and use of a comic persona—a comic tool known well by comics and jesters.

Originality and Exaggeration

We do this, in a sense, by being ourselves, by being thoroughly original, utterly and absolutely unique, and then by exaggerating our, shall we say, idiosyncrasies. That, in fact, provides the definition of a comic persona: It is an individual seizing on some aspect of her or his personal originality and then embracing whatever it is with a full-blown joyful exaggeration. But we shall try to take this apart to see how it works and how one might actually adapt it, with care and fun, for the pulpit.

First, originality. In one of his books on comedy, Gene Perret says that one of the best pieces of advice he can give about, well, his performing is to never ask him to sing:

> If you do, though, and I sing "Strangers in the Night," I'll probably sing it with hip, finger-snapping phrasing reminiscent of Frank Sinatra. If I sing, "Volare," my voice will take on the semi-intoxicated, mellifluous tones of Dean Martin. Should I sing, "To All the Girls I've Loved Before," you'll notice a nasal quality to my vocalizing, not unlike Willie Nelson. When I sing, "Rocky Mountain High," my voice soars an octave higher. John Denver would be envious. "Forever and Ever Amen" develops a definite country twang in my voice. I may even yodel a bar or two if the spirit moves me. I don't sing, "How Am I Supposed to Live Without You"; I wail it like Michael Bolton.[1]

Perret points out that he is none of those people, of course, nor is he really singing their songs. He is, however, mimicking each and every one of them. It is, in fact, this type of mimicry that prevents one from developing an original style, a style that is one's own. Someone asked the composer Sammy Cahn once how one went about writing a Sinatra song. Cahn's reply was that one didn't write a Sinatra song. He wrote a song and if and when Sinatra sang it, it became a Sinatra song. The same is true with comedy. Mimicry kills originality. One who would work with humor must do so by being completely oneself, an original. One's comic persona is one's own persona; it is neither borrowed nor copied from someone else.

It will be that way in the pulpit, as well. The preacher must be an original, copying no style, imitating no one else. This is important because one's comic persona must be completely one's own if it is to work; and even though (as we shall see) that persona may have several dimensions or may even shift over time, it must always be original. There is another reason for emphasizing this, however. It is that the comic persona of the pulpit is not a form of acting. It is not creating a character that one can play. That is what makes this different from Sam Malone's character on Cheers, or Kelsey Grammar's Frasier. In the pulpit, one is being oneself; one is not playing a made-up role. In the pulpit, instead, one is developing and embracing something that is truly oneself but deciding to have some fun with who and what that really, actually is. The difference is very important; and once that difference is well understood, the fun and originality of the comic persona can take shape.

One must not only be original, however (and we shall consider in a moment how to do that), but one must also decide—and often that is a conscious decision—not to take oneself too seriously. If one is not willing to make fun of oneself, to laugh at oneself, then the comic persona will simply not happen. One must be willing, as they say, to lighten up, to play the clown. If one can cultivate a sense of playfulness toward oneself, a playfulness in which one can engage in public—and granted, for some this is not an easy or natural thing to do—then one is ready to take the next step. That step is the process of determining what will serve as the *focus* for one's comic persona. Most comic personas arise from one of four areas of our lives, and here the preacher must do some serious introspection. The four areas are (1) some physical characteristic or quality of oneself (not somebody else); (2) some personal or situational dimension in which one lives; (3) some hobby or avocation; or (4) some intense interest that one follows whenever one is not "at work." Let us look at each of these briefly.

The Unusual Characteristic

First, for some, the comic persona might revolve around a physical characteristic that one possesses, usually an unusual characteristic, though this must, of course, be done carefully and in rigorously good taste. When comedy is taught to professionals, this is most often called a physical flaw, though that term is used in a lighthearted way. One of the preacher friends of my family when I growing up was naturally bald, completely bald, not a hair on his head. And I know from my father's stories that his baldness bothered him early in life, though he came to terms with it very quickly. Not long after he entered the ministry, he began to collect bald jokes and stories, and his collection over his life ran into the thousands, all of which he meticulously catalogued. He came to take pride in his baldness and it became his signature. He could and did talk about it—not baldness per se, for fear of offending someone else who was bald, but about *his own* baldness. It was his badge, his comic identity. His sermons could, and did, at any given point, make light of his condition. With it, he could gently and judiciously play the clown. It was never oppressive or overdone—he was very careful about that—but with a line here or one there, or a story, or a bit of good-natured bragging about his bald prowess, he could break up too much seriousness with a comic reference to his unique head. It was always funny; it always produced gentle laughter; it was always in the context of something that he wanted to say. It was his comic persona, and it served him and those who heard him preach very well. And it did not, I would emphasize, get in the way of or detract from his preaching of the gospel. In fact, it only enhanced it. He was a loved person or persona, one who knew about his baldness and chose, in effect, to celebrate it comically. He was the "bald preacher," and his attitude was clear: Would that you all were blessed as I am. It was exaggeration, a kind of incongruency. It was his comic persona. And could he preach!

In choosing a physical dimension as a basis for a comic persona, one must be careful, of course, not to engage in anything offensive. But this kind of comic persona can arise from almost anything about an individual that one might choose. It has to be something distinctive, something a bit odd, something that others do, in fact, notice. I know a preacher who is very short and very conscious of being short, as others are when they are around him. This preacher, however, treats his shortness as a special gift from God. He has made his stature his comic persona. He is able to laugh at it, to make light of it—not at others who are short, but only and always at himself. He loves to point out, even in his sermons, the difficulties that tall people have, and he constructs some wildly funny problems that afflict the over six-footers. Short people have many advantages over taller people, and he even has a Zacchaeus Gospel and a Zacchaeus theology, all well fantasized and deliciously recurrent in his sermons. It is a comic persona that he cultivates and that sprinkles lovely, gentle humor whenever he preaches. Another preacher I know is color blind, and he claims to have always been color blind. He has made his color blindness his comic persona. It is not easy to navigate through the world when you cannot tell red from green; driving can sometimes be most interesting. Or when you cannot tell whether your socks match or not, and often they don't, and you find yourself sitting on an open platform waiting to preach with socks exposed for all the world, including TV cameras, to see. One can devise a gentle comic persona, one that can be brought with originality and humor into the pulpit.

The second way in which the comic persona can be devised is based on what we might call a personal or situational dimension in which one lives, or from which one has come. Again, care must be exercised, but when this is done well, it is remarkably effective and comedic. I learned about this indirectly but then seized on it. For more than twenty-five years I was a college professor; it was my vocation, the situation of life I knew best. I came to the point, though, where I chose to leave that profession and go into the ministry full-time. No more college professoring; I found a wonderful church in which to work, one from which I would subsequently enter seminary life. But in that church, I was always the former college professor; and I decided to make that a comic persona. I could play the part of the transplanted professor, with all of the odd characteristics that are associated with college professors. I was the absent-minded professor, always absent-minded, and I could always bring a spice of the comedic into my sermons with my absent-mindedness, valued, cherished, but always getting me into or out of a jam. In addition, I know there are college professors who are neat and meticulous, but they are not me and I do not know many of them; so my messy desk and occasionally mismatched clothes also became part of my comic persona; they were things that, in an exaggerated but very serious way, I could always talk about, even from the pulpit. And, of course, there was my penchant in sermons to give "homework"—college professors get to do that, of course—homework that would consist of things that I had talked about in my sermons: "Your assignment for this week is to…oops, I forgot, I am not in that 'place' anymore, am I?" The comic persona worked. College professoring was not my position then, but that persona kept getting mixed in with what I was doing in the church. I played it that way, and people loved it. It was a funny joke, one that I made regular, though judicious, use of in my preaching.

I know a preacher who is a former attorney who does with that former profession what I did with mine. He keeps intact various comic elements that go with what lawyers are and do, the stereotypes of lawyers, and he exaggerates those stereotypes mercilessly—taking all of those exaggerated elements upon himself. He maintains that as a comic alter ego in his preaching. For example, he will sometimes in his sermons lapse into legalese—it is all planned, of course; he does it deliberately and when he does it, it is wondrously funny. It is a parody of what he was professionally, and he treats it as a very funny parody of himself. Once he gets into the legalese (which is funny in itself), he catches himself and calls himself back to "pastoral" language—and in so doing gives remarkable comic poignancy even to pastoral language and witness. There are many ways in which he does this kind of thing in the pulpit, always intentionally, always gently, but in a funny way that adds delight to the sermon.

A third kind of comic persona that can easily be taken on is based on some hobby or avocation, whatever it is. It just has to be stylized and exaggerated as well, in order to work. It must be a hobby that one, comically, good-naturedly, turns into an imaginary passion, preferably a fiery passion, a white-hot passion. Suppose we say that one's hobby is working on old cars, cars that no longer run, three of which litter one's back yard. One likes to putter with one's old cars, fixing this or changing that. Doing whatever. From that, one creates a passion for old cars and takes it upon oneself. One has a passion for such old car work because it is such an "exalted" form of work. And a discussion of the "glory" of those old cars recurs in one's sermons. In the sermon, something heavy is going on, let us say, something, well, theological. Which reminds me that I worked the other evening on the 1938 Dodge. Doesn't run yet, but I figure another four or five years and it will. I got under that hood, scraped off several layers of sixty-year-old grease, and managed to get that spark plug out. Or whatever. And there will be a connection—one can usually find a metaphorical connection of some sort that can be made—with the theology. Can the 1938 Dodge rise again? Of course. Absolutely. Prayer, a lot of hard work, and the constant scraping of grease—miracles happen, but not without the loving care of one who really cares about that Dodge. The preacher identifies with those old cars, masterpieces in their heyday—they don't make them like that anymore. And it is sort of like…well, the imagination takes over; the comic persona does its work. And people get to know the old cars and the humor of the preacher's comic persona.

The Society of Cats

Over the years for me, animals have been a kind of hobby. I got into rescuing animals, particularly birds and cats. At one point, there were more than a dozen cats calling our house "home." We knew them by name, even by personality. I thoroughly enjoyed feeding them and watching their reactions, not only to me but to so many things in the outbuildings where they lived. Every night, to make sure they were all accounted for, I would open a large can of tuna and parcel out little bits of tuna to each one of them. They would cluster around me and climb all over me to get their tuna. One had to work to keep them apart so that even the smallest and scrawniest of them would get a few of those morsels. Those cats became part of my preaching. I valued the cats. But in order for my persona to become a cat persona, I exaggerated not just their role in my life but their own personalities and interactions. I made those cats real. I brought them to life. I turned their "society" metaphorically into a human society, since I came to know theirs quite well. They helped in my preaching. I was the preacher with the cats. But those cats on many occasions, sometimes with just a line in passing in the sermon, sometimes with a story, provided metaphor after metaphor of human action and interaction. I would look at the human world through the perspective of the "cat world," as I understood it, and the human world took on new dimensions as a result of that perspective. It was a hobby that I stylized into a cat persona, one that I enjoy and value to this day.

The fourth area that often provides the basis for a workable comic persona is not a hobby or an avocation, but it is something that one simply "likes to do." One exaggerates it then into something that one likes to do a lot, but that also is intensely *worth doing*; and this is where the fun of the activity kicks in. One surrounds the activity with an aura. Let's say the preacher likes soap operas on television—I'm making all of this up. Schedules are full, but I, the preacher, always try to build my daily schedule around them, and when I cannot be there from 1:00 to 3:00 in the afternoon—people do, can you believe it, expect me to work those hours some days—I keep the timer on the television doing its thing; so I can keep up in the evening at least. Soaps keep me in touch with who I am and with what the "real people" of the world are living through. Soaps have a way of bringing people together. One must like the soaps to do this, of course, but the comic persona here is based on exaggerating that liking into a full-blown, tongue-in-cheek religion of soap opera. Or it may be that one likes to go to the stock car races, does every now and then. It's a weird interest, but it could happen. One could easily turn that liking into a wonderfully comic persona, describing all of the "wonders" of the event and, being quite specific though exaggerated, describing from time to time the experience of "being there." Or one might like to read mystery novels. That, too, with exaggeration and some ultra-serious detail, could become a working comic persona.

This was also illustrated well, but from a different perspective, by one of my Claremont students in the class which I taught on comedy and preaching some time back. She was a young woman, a third-year student, a newlywed who made the weekly trips to school from her home in Phoenix. She had been married about a year, was surrounded not only by her own large, loving family, but now by her new husband's large and loving family—all of whom lived not more than a few miles from where she and her husband were settling down. She was in love not only with her new husband, her own family and his, but with the very idea of being married. It infused everything she did. You could see it in her face, her actions, her personality. She decided to let us see it in her preaching as well. Quite deliberately, her comic persona for preaching became that of the deliriously happy new bride. She was happy, of course, but she picked up ways to exaggerate it into a wonderfully comic range. There was nothing cynical about her exaggeration, as so much marriage comedy is these days. In fact, what she did was exactly right for the pulpit. It was a twinkle in the eye kind of exaggeration, the kind that said, of course we all know that it will not always be like this; it fact, it probably isn't exactly like this now, but it is what I always dreamed about in my storybook worlds of childhood. He is my white knight. He can do no wrong; I don't care what he does with his socks. I don't have to worry about fixing him, since there is nothing to fix; and I know that as he gets older, he will want to spend even less time than he does now watching sports on TV.

In one's preaching, one discusses one's comic "passion," a little bit here, a little bit there, a little more in a later sermon. One uses the comic passion as a way of talking about other things, the serious things. The comic passion becomes a metaphor, exaggerated, elongated, stretched, but not out of bounds. The Christian faith is like one of the cars that I work on in my back yard. Lot of people around me, my neighbors, don't like those cars there. Call them eyesores. But they don't see their beauty like I do. Last week after I got back from calling on people at the hospital, I put on my old clothes and went out to work on one of those cars... And off one goes. In next Sunday's sermon there will probably be a way to make some use of the "old cars" or the "soap operas" or "my well-near ideal kids." And the following week they might be taken into account again, though I guess we could take a week off, despite the sheer importance (and lessons) of those cars, or soaps, or kids, or whatever. And the preacher, without even trying, develops a comic persona. To mention the cars in a sermon, to discuss some new aspect of metaphor of the old cars becomes funny, comic. People delight in it. Can it get old? Of course, and one must go about it all very carefully not to let that happen. One must not overdo it. That would do nothing but spoil the fun.

Two questions, however, remain about the nature of the comic persona as it is brought into the pulpit. The first is whether a preacher's persona can be, as they say, too far out; and the answer is a decided "yes." One must choose a persona very carefully, keeping close to kinds of personalities that are well known, that are both genuine and gentle, and that are easily recognizable by the congregants with whom one preaches. One cannot go to the outer fringes of society, however one defines that, in order to devise a comic persona for the pulpit. The comic persona can and should be distinctive and even somewhat quirky, but in a good-natured way, always; and in a way that is not foreign to those who must share it. It is an important caution.

The second question is also very practical, and it revolves around the question of whether the preacher can have multiple comic personas? The answer, as with so many questions, is both a yes and a no. The "no" is to indicate that the preacher would be well advised to cultivate only one comic persona at a time, or at least one dominant one. Two can work, if one is more important than the other and if they are kept in a gentle balance. In my experience, I have had an animal, a cat and bird, persona, one that I made consistent and dominant use of. At the same time, I was the "college professor" that I described earlier, too. The two did not interfere with each other, and in fact they provided a way to stretch out their use over time. And both worked. There may be interests that for a preacher are lifelong, and those may very well, if handled with restraint and consistency, extend over a lifetime in the pulpit. The preacher becomes known in the pulpit as this kind of person or that one, this kind of comic persona or that one. For some preachers, perhaps for many who take seriously the things we have said here, that will not only become a hallmark of ministry and effective, delightful preaching, but also a way to give a ministry the distinctiveness and public visibility that the pulpit, particularly in mainstream Protestantism, could use a lot more of.

The "yes" of the question, though, is that the preacher may, over periods of time, go through changes that lend themselves very well to a shifting of comic personas. My student, the young newlywed who for some time could assume that unique identity as a comic persona may, at some point in the not-too-distant future, move out of that persona and into another, perhaps as a mother, taking up that comic identity and letting that become the basis for the playfulness that she brings to her preaching. And then, even, when her children are teenagers, another comic persona could take shape. I am not holding her in any way to "family" imagery as a basis for her comic personae of the future, but seeing it that way indicates the nature of the changes through which one might go as one's pulpit ministry develops over time.

We need to return to the theological issue with which we began: Does the comic persona, as we have examined it, interfere in any way with the preacher's preaching of the gospel? The answer is no; when the comic persona is done judiciously and with good humor, it not only does not hinder the gospel—it dramatically enhances it. When there is no fun in the pulpit, where the seriousness is unrelenting and even cloying, the gospel is somehow diminished. It is diminished not only because the joy is drained from it, but because, in our time at least, people will not be easily drawn into, or long remain involved in, either its form or its presentation.

We are hungry today for people to be drawn to church, drawn into the sanctuary, into what Reinhold Niebuhr years ago called the "holy of holies"; but they are only going to be drawn in where there is a spirit of joy and celebration, where the comic spirit pervades, and where comic personas, like court jesters of old, send out the call and offer warmth and celebration to all who will come. The comic persona is not contrary to the gospel; in fact, the gospel itself needs comic personas in order for its speaking to be both inviting and invigorating. For those who have both the courage and the sensitivity to bring the spirit of play and playfulness into the pulpit, the rewards, to both the church and the gospel, will be remarkable indeed.

PART III

The Comic Sermon in the Pulpit

9

The Constructing of a Comic Sermon

A sermon is not a comic sermon because it is funny or because it causes people to laugh, as important as those things can sometimes be. It is a comic sermon because it deals with subjects, with life, or even with scripture, in a comic way. It reflects the kind of complex comic dimensions that we discussed in the previous chapters. The sermon may be funny and people may laugh, of course; and one might even hope for that to take place. But that is not the *mark* of the comic sermon. Sermons are serious business, as every preacher knows; and comic sermons are serious business as well, as odd as that may sound. The questions at this point are: What *makes* a sermon a comic sermon? How does one, in fact, go about the preparation of such a sermon? How, too, does one find that delicate balance between the comic and the "serious"?

Earlier, I contended that the resurgence of humor, or the comedic, in the pulpit coincides with the emergence of new theologies—of what we have called postmodern theologies. It is my contention that these developments are not coincidental: Comedy

141

is fundamentally immanent, as are the various postmodern theologies, despite their otherwise considerable variation. The postmodern theologies, whether process, narrative, or some variation of one of these, foster the comedic vision. The rise of the comedic in preaching also coincides with the emergence, as gradual as it is, of a new kind of preaching, a *postmodern preaching*. Neither is this coincidental. The outlines of this new kind of preaching have emerged rather clearly over the past two decades or so, under various names and designations. There is no way, however, in my view, to understand the nature of the comedic sermon without grasping its connection to the postmodern sermon. This is because the comedic sermon is, by its nature, a postmodern sermon. Hence, while this book is not designed to be a full study of postmodern preaching, some discussion of the postmodern sermon is necessary for us to grasp the place and the method of the comedic in it.

The postmodern sermon is characterized by at least three fundamental changes from preaching of the preceding eras—controversial changes as far as homiletics is concerned, but no less controversial than the assertion that comedy has a crucial role to play in preaching.

The first of these three changes concerns the sermon's relation to the biblical text. What we will call, for want of a better term, modern preaching saw (sees) the sermon's chief function to be the *reiteration* of the biblical text in some creative, memorable fashion. The message of the sermon was the message of the text, plain and simple. Before the 1980s, that meant that the content of the sermon was to be the content of the text, even though there were various forms that the content could take. In the early 1980s, that idea was modified somewhat to incorporate both content and form; this meant that the sermon was obligated to replicate *both* the content and the form of the text.

In the 1990s, however, advocates for the postmodern sermon have contended for a different view of the biblical text, at least as far as preaching text is concerned. Not surprisingly, as we indicated in the previous chapter, the comic sermon shares the view of text held by the postmodern sermon. Here, the idea is that the biblical text is not so much to be reiterated as it is to be examined and interacted with in the sermon. This, in fact, as we have already seen, is what allows the text to be part of the comic spirit in preaching. The text may be heard and listened to, of course; but the text may also be challenged and evaluated as well. In the postmodern sermon the text, in short, may be heard, but it must also make room for other voices, other experiences, and other forms of community-building as well. The authority for the preacher's speaking lies not so much in the biblical text itself in postmodern theology and homiletics; it arises much more from the larger context in which both preacher and community live, work, and worship.

The Change in Sermon Sources

The second change from the modern to the postmodern sermon—not unrelated to the place of the biblical text—has to do with the sources of material for the sermon. The sermon—the comic sermon as well as the postmodern sermon—draws its material not from the Bible or the biblical text alone, as it tended to do until relatively recently; it draws its material, instead, from wherever it can find it. The text may, of course, be part of the sermon—even, in some cases, its pivotal dimension; a sermon's comic sense may arise from the sermon's text. But the postmodern, and the comic sermon, may draw just as readily from current news events, historical events long past or relatively recent, popular arts or culture, and, particularly, on the preacher's own experiences and recollections, the preacher's own stories. In the postmodern sermon, these elements are not peripheral to the text, not just what used to be called illustrative; together with biblical material, they make up the very text of the sermon itself.

In one of his early essays on the nature of postmodern thought, the French philosopher Jacques Derrida called attention to the anthropological studies of Ferdinand Levi-Strauss. What Levi-Strauss devised, Derrida noted, was a method of work that resembled what the French call *bricolage*, or the process of collecting and using whatever materials are at hand; whatever, literally, is lying on the ground.[1] One creates by gathering and fitting together odds and ends, bits and pieces, some of this and some of that, none of which was made for the use to which it is put, but from which something new and novel can be devised. It results in something assembled from found objects, something created, as it were, out of nothing. For Derrida, the postmodern writer fashions writing in the same way: by gathering odds and ends, bits and pieces, found things, from many places. By the same token, the postmodern preacher becomes a gatherer of bits and pieces from many places for the fashioning of a sermon. One of those bits and pieces is, invariably, a biblical text, and it may even on occasion be the formative piece; but it does not, in the postmodern sermon, have to be.

The third change in postmodern and comic preaching is that it represents a new form of logic, or, more accurately, a new approach to the very idea of logic. It is not based on the Aristotelian logic of deduction or progression. It is not based on causal relationship; that is, if the first thing is true, it leads to the second, which leads to the third, and so on. It is not based on the logic of argumentation: this is true because all of the following things are true. It is based, instead, on a logic (if we choose to call it that) of juxtaposition. It is the logic of relationship. Things, pieces, are not related to each other causally, no matter what the nature of the hierarchy; they are related to each other because one chooses to establish, or discover, relationships.

This is the logic of film montage, which is the art of placing unrelated, or seemingly unrelated, sections of film end to end without any "transitions." It is running ten seconds of film of a speeding locomotive followed by ten seconds of a woman pushing a baby carriage, followed by eight seconds of the locomotive and then eight seconds of the woman and her carriage, followed by five seconds of the speeding locomotive, then five seconds of the woman and her carriage. By this time, the viewers are seeing, or rather creating, a definite relationship between the speeding locomotive and the woman and her baby carriage, a relationship where none inherently, or logically, exists. The viewers, though, with no prompting whatever, even know—or at least they think they do—how the two sets of sequences are related. The locomotive is going to hit…well, we don't have to give it away. It is the logic that says when two things are placed together within a common setting, or when they are arranged in some kind of sequential order—as in film or a sermon, they must, somehow, be related. The task in hearing (or viewing) is to uncover or discover the nature of the relationship. The hearer/viewer/participant, though, is the one who must, as it were, discover that relationship. It is understood, moreover, that whoever created the montage probably had something in mind during the creative process, even though what the participant in that montage creates from the juxtaposed pieces may or may not correspond very well to the creator's vision of it.

This is the principle that lies at the core of what we mean by inductive thinking, whatever it is applied to, including the sermon. Pieces are selected, arranged by some principle of the creator's devising—which can take many forms, of course—and then laid end to end so that, when taken together, what they are designed to do or say emerges only gradually. This is not just inductive thinking or logic. It is also the approach to creativity that, more than anything else, has come to define the postmodern sensibility. In the older, or "modern" forms, focusing again on the sermon, the deductive process was the norm, with the central idea or affirmation (usually called a proposition, after the debating model) clearly stated up front and the rest of the presentation devoted to a polemical argument of some kind in support of that affirmation. That has now changed. The respected homiletician Richard Eslinger has put it like this:

> Unlike the essay model, with its relatively seamless and free-flowing development, most homiletic methods sharing a postcritical perspective are episodic in some way or other…In fact, a new language is being developed by biblical interpreters and homileticians to speak of these surface-level episodes in Scripture and in preaching—"moves," "lexies," and "stages" are three of the labels given to these sermon components. Whatever our method, we are more likely to be forming a plot composed of these episodes than we are to be assembling points, themes, and sub-themes.[2]

Sermons, then, are devised by episodes, set in juxtaposition—sequences is the term that I now use to talk about these sections. Eslinger adds that for an oral, sermonic address to be heard and retained by the postmodern congregation, "it must be designed in the congregational hearing as relatively brief components-in-sequence," components that "will all have a relationship to each other that the preacher shapes." While these sermons will "differ in specifics," they will all be "episodic and inherently mobile, reflecting some notion of a homiletic plot."[3]

The Television Sensibility

While Eslinger, along with postmodern (or postcritical) preachers, are gradually coming to terms with this juxtapositional, sequential process in which components, often unrelated on their surface, are laid together to create logic rather than to reflect it, this has been the model of television sensibility throughout the 1990s. I write this only a few weeks after the announcement that Jerry Seinfeld is ending his wildly successful sitcom after nine years—an announcement that made page one of the *Los Angeles Times,* which called the program the "pop culture touchstone" of the decade. In his lament—not review—of the comedy that day, *Times* television critic Howard Rosenberg wrote: "Pulling the plug on a masterpiece of nothingness that epitomizes the sitcom as art? One that in episode after episode has been uproarious in the way it seams together seemingly unrelated subplots—that are not just far-fetched but out-of-sight-fetched—in such absurdly contrived ways that you can see the jagged stitches?"[4] Seinfeld caught that "structural" genius of the ultimately postmodern decade: sections of various lives, intertwined but not intertwined, stitched together in such a way that the viewer has to be party to making the juxta-positions work, if they are going to work at all. The comedy was in the stitching, the sewing together of incongruity. Such an aes-thetic has not left the sermon unaffected, and the new forms of sermon-making that Eslinger describes reflect this sequential montage, not just a montage of technique, but a montage as well of sermonic content.

Grasping these kinds of changes is essential if we are to get a sense of how the comedic becomes part and parcel with the postmodern sermon. But we can readily illustrate these changes by examining again the sermon by Fred Craddock reproduced in the appendix, the sermon titled, "When the Roll Is Called Down Here." It is, in my judgment, an example of a postmodern ser-mon, as I have outlined it here. The sermon is easily broken down into sections, or sequences, as I have done with simple lines. In my counting there are nine sequences, plus a few lines of intro-duction, which, for some, may count as a tenth sequence. Look at them carefully, first, to see the sermon's unique construction. The sequences are laid end to end. Some of them are connected by a short sentence, a transitional sentence, most are not. In some cases, the transition is nothing more than the simple, repeated line: Don't call it a list; it is not a list.

Now, look at the sequences: (1) jury duty; (2) Paul calling the roll—from the text; (3) background about Paul; (4) remembering the quilt; (5) humanizing the characters in Paul's list; (6) the Viet-nam list in Atlanta; (7) Paul saying "goodbye—text; (8) Make a list of your own, an intriguing sequence that is split into two parts, the second half becoming the end of the sermon; right in the middle of the two halves is (9) the Watts Bar Lake baptism story. Three of the nine sequences are from or about the text: Numbers 2, 5 and 7. But the rest of the sequences are drawn from here and there, in the bricoleur's fashion. The other sequences are not "illustrations" of the text; they are, if anything, elaborations of it, extensions of it. Or maybe the text is an extension of various pieces that the preacher brings to the sermon. The sequences are cobbled together, stuck together with the duct tape of a juxtapositional logic and a wonderfully repeated line. Nothing seems to dictate which piece goes where or how it will contribute to the whole. And the sequences have come from different places in the preacher's experience: from a recent trip to jury duty, from a trip in time past to see a replica of the Vietnam Wall, from two experiences early in the preacher's ministry, and from, of all places, the preacher's own imaginative story-making capacity. The ending story is made-up, fictitious. But it works. Here is the preacher as bricoleur, collecting odds and ends, a piece here and a piece there, fishing around in one's own imagination and recollection, fashioning items from nearby and from far away, as far as time is concerned. It is a postmodern way of thinking and a postmodern way of constructing a sermon.

This sermon, though, is also a comic sermon, one that presses the line between laughter and tears. But the sermon is not comic because of its subject, or even its subject matter. In fact, the Craddock sermon we are examining is about a very serious and important subject, which is the need for people, and particularly Christians, to stay close, as it were, to all of those who have shaped or influenced one's life or ministry. No one is self-made. Everyone has been helped along life's path, not by one or two people, but by numerous individuals. And one must never forget them. Not only must one never forget them, one must from time to time single them out, thank them, touch someone else in the name of one who has touched oneself. This is a serious sermon that wants to say something the preacher believes to be very important, something motivated by scripture, but which is in no way a reiteration of the Romans 16 text. It is a play on the text, an interaction, at best, with it. Still, the sermon, at its base, is not an effort to be funny. It is not a comic topic. One does not, in other words, set out to find a funny subject for a sermon. One does not try to leave scripture behind in order, this week, to preach a funny sermon. It does not work that way. While there may be times when what the sermon is about may embody a humorous element, it is not that sermon idea that usually creates the comic dimension in preaching.

When Sequences Are Comic

At its most basic level, though, a sermon becomes comic when some, though not usually all, of its *bricolaged* sequences are comic in nature. Comic here may not mean funny in any overt sense, but may mean that the stories or sequences are humorous by virtue of their sheer humanity, their sketching of human foible and/or encounter. One cannot, either, draw a line between the biblical text sequences as being the serious ones and the nonbiblical sequences being the comic ones; we have examined ways of creating comic elements from biblical text. In the case of the Craddock sermon, for example, the two most *serious* pieces are one of each, one from life and one from the text, and they come back to back. One sees the first in the comments about the Vietnam Wall, which tend to call up tears, followed immmediately by the sequence of Paul, saying goodbye. He's not saying hello, he is saying goodbye; now pray with me, agonize with me. But there are other serious sequences, even though the comic is not far under the surface in any of them. The serious ones are Paul's rundown of the list in sequence 2, another is sequence 3, and even sequence 4, the story about the quilt, about remembering the names on the quilt.

The comic sequences, though, are clear and well spaced. They begin with the jury duty story, a funny piece in a very wry way. Next would be the text sequences (2, 5, and 7) where the preacher humanizes the names in Paul's list. It is done imaginatively, of course; but with a deeply humorous set of details. And then there are the two pieces, interwoven to form the end of the sermon, the Watts Bar Lake baptism story, and the story of the people waiting inside heaven's gate. Both are very funny sequences, the Watts Bar Lake baptism story, which, interestingly, matches in both flavor and form the jury duty story that opens the sermon, and the "keep your list" story, a wildly contrived story that is both funny and poignant at the same time.

The point is that a comic sermon becomes comic when *some* of the sequences in a serious sermon are comic sequences. All of them do not have to be; in fact, all of them probably *should* not be. The comic sequences, though, provide a kind of seasoning that creates the flavor of the sermon, that sets it in a comic space and invites people into that space. The comic sequences, by their very power, provide the sermon with two strong qualities. First, they set up an aura for the sermon, a sense of joy, delight, and surprise that surrounds the sermon. We may be caught at any time, the comic sequences promise, in a twist of laughter or light-heartedness. The matter taken up in the sermon may be serious, and we do not miss that; but there is the possibility of humor always around the corner. It is an anticipation that shapes even the more serious thinking that the sermon may offer. Second, the comic sequences implicitly, but unmistakably, set up the theological framework for the sermon, a framework usually drawn, whether deliberately or not, from the new postmodern theological positions of immanence. The comic sequences are "this world" sequences, not as sermon application, but as stories that embody the presence and working out of God in human life.

In the case of the Craddock sermon, the comic pieces are stories, however real or contrived they may be. The jury pool story has humans reflecting together on names and identities; the quilt story is a story of moving and remembering, of taking a remembrance along on the move over time and space; the Watts Bar Lake baptism story is a story from the past, of real church, as contrived as the story itself actually sounds. Even the concluding sequence, the list taken to heaven, while it is an imaginative creation about heaven, is about things right here on earth after all. It centers around a group of people preparing a welcome home party, big sign draped over the street and all. It is a very "this worldly" imaginative story, transferred to heaven. Where do these stories come from? They are all made up, though their seeds arise from the closely watched experiences of and by the preacher. By calling the stories "made up" we mean that they are very stylized, as we described earlier. They are based on an idea or an experience, on some memory, and then the stories are "constructed" or molded like clay to fit into this particular sermon. One can easily imagine that the same stories could be told in other sermons on other subjects, but that each story would be told in a different way, one that would reflect the needs of that particular sermon.

Guidelines for Comic Sequences

There are six guidelines that, if followed, will greatly assist the preacher in creating and incorporating comic sequences into a sermon, that will enable the preacher, in effect, to devise and preach effective—and fun—comic sermons. The first is that comic sequences must *fit* the sermon into which they are placed. Sermons are not built around comic pieces, but, instead, sermons are built around themes or topics, whether picked randomly or devised from texts—"I want the sermon to say this"—and then the comic sequences are designed to contribute in some way to that theme or topic. After the sermon topic is selected and some statement of the topic is worked out, the preacher must usually brainstorm intensely, searching in the files of thought and memory for stories or even pieces of stories that might actually fit with what he or she wants to say. Earlier, we talked about maintaining one's story files. In many cases, one's brainstorming notes in preparation for a sermon—and one should develop a habit of making notes during such brainstorming sessions—may contain eight, ten, a dozen, or even more separate potential pieces from which comic stories or sequences might be fashioned. The task, then, is to discard and discard until the very best sequences are fashioned into a clean fit for the sermon.

The second guideline is that each comic sequence must not only fit, but must make its own unique and well-defined contribution to the sermon, both imaginatively and consciously. This means that each sequence, but particularly each comic sequence, must be different from all of the other sequences in the contribution it makes to the overall sermon. One can sometimes be inclined to incorporate a series of sequences, or stories, particularly comic stories, in a sermon, because they are all nice, because they fit. Often, though, these stories are fundamentally alike, or they end up saying the same thing, and so a kind of repetition develops, one that is readily spotted by the sermon's sharers. In selecting comic stories or sequences for the sermon, the preacher must look carefully at each chosen sequence to ask what makes it different from every other sequence, and what unique contribution to the sermon it makes. If one looks back again at Craddock's sequences—or even at our listing of the sequences earlier—one sees clearly that each sequence does something very specific that no other sequence does; each sequence, that is, *advances* the sermon carefully toward its conclusion, not "logically," but thematically and relationally. In one sense, this kind of sermon may be conceptualized as a finely cut diamond held up to a light. Every surface on the diamond sparkles in a different way, and each one makes its own contribution to the beauty of the overall gem. So must the pieces, the sequences, of the comic sermon be.

The third guideline is that comic sequences should be judiciously spaced throughout the sermon. In postmodern preaching, sermons will usually have between seven and ten sequences, some of which will be specifically comic. Often the first or the first couple of sequences may be comic ones, and there is certainly a naturalness about that. Sometimes the opening sequence will be a text-based one, but handled in a comic manner, as we discussed in an earlier chapter. There should be some spacing, though, between the comic sequences and those that are not comic. Another look at Craddock's sermon will remind one of how he has spaced the comic sequences through the sermon. It is unusual, and very difficult, for a sermon to end with a comic sequence, as the Craddock sermon here does. The preacher will usually want to end, shall we say, on a serious note rather than a comic one. What should be understood, however, is that when the concluding sequence is a comic one, and when it fits well into the flow of the sermon's sequences, few things are more powerful or more satisfying to those who share the sermon. To laugh or to feel a surge of joy at the end of the sermon—and to get the point of the sermon at the same time—is to achieve a climactic moment in preaching that is rare and exquisite indeed.

The fourth guideline is to let sequences, including the comic ones, that are different from each other stand in juxtaposition with each other. Just let them stand next to each other, or wrapped around each other (in a sense), without any particular effort to explain how or why one is doing so. Saying this sounds as though it would be disjointed or confusing, but in reality neither is the case. One should remember that the very best of the television situation comedies, like *Seinfeld* or *Frasier*, have pioneered a new way of story-making; that is, the writers set up two and sometimes three story lines that run concurrently. The story lines are related, of course, but are tangential to each other, and it is up to the viewer to make connections and fill in gaps, something that human beings of whatever educational level seem perfectly able and more than willing to do. The strands, or sequences, overlap, and we watch for the moments of overlap. When we find them, we are able to fill in the off-camera goings-on of the characters, and we enjoy the process of doing so.

While this is not exactly the process of creating the postmodern sermon, the dynamics of speaking and hearing are roughly the same. We set up our sequences as various strains of the story we are telling, of what we are wanting to say in the sermon. They are related, of course, but they are also tangential to each other, and those who share what we say and how we say it are asked—or invited—to fill in the gaps and enjoy the points of intersection or overlap. There is a comic dimension, often a very compelling one, in the nature of the juxtapositions we establish. In the Craddock sermon, this is concisely illustrated with the last two sequences, the ones that are intercut with each other. On their surface, they are absolutely unrelated to each other; and, in fact, the hearers could conceivably become confused. "Do you have a piece of paper? Well, use your worship bulletin. Would you write in the margin somewhere or at the bottom these words..." You choose a name. Write another, and another. Why? Wait a minute? OK, but what am I doing this for? This is a game, isn't it? "Before I married and was serving a little mission in the Appalachians..." Yes, of course it is a game. To the end of the story: "In that community, their name for that is *church*. They call that church." Then: "Have you written any names? Do you have a name or two?"

It is a form of cutting, of editing. Transitions? No, there are none. Yet no one gets lost or confused, because we are, in fact, used to this kind of "logic." It is the logic of montage that we discussed a few minutes ago, carried from the physical cutting and splicing of film to the very process of story—and sermon—making. The comedy is in the cutting. It is in the challenge of waiting, of figuring things out, of knowing that there is an unexpectedness to all this, a sense of surprise. That is where the fun of it all lies in wait.

The fifth guideline may be called a theological one, though no less a comic one as far as the arrangement of the sermon's sequences is concerned. This is because a comic dimension is present when one sets up one's sequences, *not to resolve theological ambiguity, but to enhance it*. We are accustomed to think that there is only confusion in ambiguity, and that can, of course, be true. But we also know that when lines become too well drawn, when everything becomes too firm and sure, when everything is thoroughly spelled out, it is the comic who must teach us, as it were, that the world is not as neat and fixed as we might like it to be. One must leave holes, theological ones. One must tweak theological certainties, and one does that by letting sermon sequences, particularly comic ones, stand on their own. Transitions, efforts to tie sequences neatly together, are not always necessary or even desirable. It is not uncommon in a postmodern sermon to move from one sequence to another without any transition whatever. There can be transitions, to be sure; and in the Craddock sermon one finds a few simple statements that appear to be transitional in nature. But there is a sense of having no transitions in the sermon as well; or with movement from one sequence to the next simply signaled, which is what the recurring line, "Don't call it a list," does for the sermon.

Is this risky for the preacher? In a sense, of course it is. It creates ambiguity about what the sermon is saying, about what it means. Is Craddock's sermon about remembering the past and those who were there an ambiguous sermon? Is it about giving thanks to God for those who helped? Is it about giving thanks, one by one, to those who helped? Is it about the nature of the church, as the Watts Bar Lake baptism story suggests? If it is about the church, then what does the preacher actually believe about the church, about what it is like? The Watts Bar Lake story is a comic one, but it is profoundly ambiguous—and the preacher does not appear to feel compelled to explain it. The bottom line is that the sermon is, in remarkable ways, ambiguous and yet not ambiguous. Like so many of Craddock's sermons, it is not just open-ended at the end; it has open windows all along the way where people can either climb in or jump out. A closer look suggests, moreover, that the sermon is rife with theological overtones and assumptions, but they all seem to stay below the surface, just out of sight. They are never quite clarified, and the distinct impression is that the preacher has—or had—no inclination to try to clarify them. In fact, there seems to be in the sermon a studied refusal to clarify the ecclesiology of it all. It is, in fact, the ambiguity that one takes from the sermon. It is also the ambiguity—in the midst of very concrete storytelling—that gives the sermon, at least in part, its strong comic flavor.

Arranging by Playfulness

Finally, there is in the arrangement of the sequences a sheer playfulness, something that also characterizes not only the comic sermon but also the postmodern sermon. Craddock's sermon is serious, one does not miss that, and yet it is devised in a decidedly non-serious fashion. It is also a profoundly biblical sermon, neither can that be missed; and yet even in that there is an unmistakable non-seriousness. There is no attempt, overt or otherwise, to be funny; and yet the preacher clearly wants to have a good time, one even bordering on mischief. The sermon takes chances, but they are playful chances, the kinds of chances involved in hollering that one is going to jump out of this playground swing at this unbelievable height. And I can do it, too. Watch.

The idea of play has become a much-explored concept in postmodern thought. Since Johan Huizinga first published his groundbreaking *Homo Ludens: A Study of the Play-Element in Culture* in the early 1950s (the first English edition, published by Beacon Press), sociologists and anthropologists have thought about the central role of play in human action and community. *Homo ludens* means "the human who plays." Other European philosophers picked up the idea in the 1960s, taking it as a central metaphor for language and community, and for the breakdown of both.[5] The work ethic, which has shaped Western culture since the Enlightenment, has been replaced with the play ethic, at least as far as postmodernism is concerned. It is a throwback to the beginnings of human activity. Huizinga began his book with this striking paragraph:

> Play is older than culture, for culture, however inadequately defined, always presupposes human society, and animals have not waited for man to teach them their playing. We can safely assert, even, that human civilization has added no essential feature to the general idea of play. Animals play just like men. We have only to watch young dogs to see that all of the essentials of human play are present in their merry gambols. They invite one another to play by a certain ceremoniousness of attitude and gesture. They keep to the rule that you shall not bite, or not bite hard, your brother's ear. They pretend to get terribly angry. And—what is most important— in all these doings they plainly experience tremendous fun and enjoyment.[6]

What Huizinga pointed out, and what Derrida, among others, has followed up on, is that play has not one meaning, but numerous meanings, all of which bear on this extraordinary phenomenon. For example, to even talk about play, or playing, is to talk about non-serious behavior. It is to talk about having fun, about laughing and cutting up, about joking and romping, about biting each other, but not too hard. It is about taunts of "I dare you" and "no you can't" and "yes I can," about game-playing, about winning and losing, about starting and stopping, and about giving one's absolute best for some inherently inconsequential activity. It is about being a child. It is child-like behavior, and it is childish behavior. Except you become as a little child, you cannot know what playing is like; at least, you cannot after you have reached a certain age of adulthood.

The idea of play, though, is dramatically more complex than that. As Derrida has pointed out, to talk about play is to talk about the space between things, about the nature of give. Let out some more play on that line, is the way one might say it, and we all know what that means. It means that something is not fixed tightly; it is not pulled taut. It means that some may take something one way, and some another. It means that just when something appears to be a sure thing, it is not. There is give in it, play in it. But there is more to it than that, even. We talk about giving a play or seeing a play, by which we mean something that is real even though it is make-believe. It is something acted out on a stage or in a round. It is the fine art of "let's pretend." It is the suspension of real belief in order to explore other forms of belief or real belief. I'll be the king and you be the queen. I'll say you have to obey me, and you say, "No, I don't." To pretend is to engage in real behavior, of course, but it is behavior at a distance. It is agreeing that something is real when everyone knows it is not, and that it is OK for it not to be real. In fact, we are able to come to terms with certain things by creating a "let's pretend" world, the world of the play.

All of this comes to bear on the postmodern sermon, which, from this perspective, becomes a form of play, or playing. That is its root, in fact. To preach here is to have fun, not only in the pulpit but also in the preparation for the pulpit. It is serious fun, as we have said, but it is fun, nevertheless. It is the fun of becoming aware in sermon preparation of the jury experience, then deciding to bring it to the pulpit. It is the fun of playing in one's mind and in one's study with the Watts Bar Lake story, the fun of reliving it, or recreating it, of making a new sandcastle out of it, and deciding to bring it into the pulpit so that the play inherent in it is continued and shared. It is the child rummaging in a old toy chest; or of returning to a playground where, in one's distant past, one would go to play in the sand and swing on the swings. The sand is now dirty and the swings are rusty, but they can still be enjoyed. They bring back memories, and yet they still speak to the present. In fact, they create the child of the past in a present moment. And in that creation, or re-creation, they have things to say to the adult child of the now.

In preparing the sermon, too, we are writing a play. It has acts and scenes. The curtain comes down here and goes up there. The audience is involved in it. There are characters and frames of dialogue and action. It is a performance, this sermon. It cannot not be. We are no longer afraid to call preaching a form of performance, something that takes place on a small stage; a performance art is what some homileticians are now beginning to see in it. It is not to be artificial, because a good play on stage is never artificial. It is make-believe, but it is good make-believe. It is believable make-believe. That is what the postmodern sermon can be. We will act out the sermon in a believable way, as reflecting what is really going on with us as preachers, but we have fun in the process.

The comic sermon can also participate in make-believe, as odd as that sounds. We can make things up, not to mislead or be untrue in some way, but in the way that one makes up a novel or a good story. Look again at the ending of Prof. Craddock's sermon. It is make-believe. It makes a point, one strong enough to stand at the end of the sermon. But it is imaginary. It is true; it is real; it works. But it is thoroughly playful. It is the kid dressing up and making up a story to explain the strange clothes. It is a real thing we are doing in our sermon, but we will, from time to time, pretend. It probably will not come out that way, unless we say we want it to, of course; and yet we will often do it. Stories we tell will have a "once upon a time" quality to them. We may say they happened to us, or that we experienced them, but we will be telling the stories as children tell stories to each other: haltingly, and with a mixture of fact and fantasy, along with a dash of how we wish the story had been. It will have a quality of "and then this happened, and then that happened, and then this happened"— we will string the pieces together and they will hold together because we say they are supposed to hold together. It is the sequence process done in a childlike manner, and everyone will not only recognize that that is the case, but will find joy and even mirth in the process. If one were now to re-read the sermon by Craddock one would discover—if one wanted to—all of those different flavors of what Huizinga called the "play-element." These are guidelines only for the constructing of a sequential sermon, a comic sermon. They are not "rules," since no two preachers will carry out this preparatory process in the same way. Everyone must, in fact, get his or her own sense of how to respond to the tasks involved here. We are, however, now ready to preach our comic sermon.

10

The Art of Preaching
a Comic Sermon

The sermon is prepared. It is a comic sermon, and it is time to take it into the pulpit or onto the platform. We want it to be effective. We want it to work, however we conceive of the idea of working. We want the same comic spirit that infused our preparation of the sermon to infuse the communication of that sermon when we deliver it. So what do we need to know about how to get that done with our comic sermon? To answer that question, though, let's turn it a different direction. Let's ask what the preacher might learn from those who teach and perform as professional comedians, those who train and practice the fine art of stand-up comedy.

For a long time, I have been a fan of the comedy clubs that sprang up all over the country in the 1970s. What started out as bars featuring some comic entertainment gradually became places of comedy entertainment with bars. One gradually paid more for the comedy than for the drinks, and in not a few such establishments soft drinks—OK, high-priced soft drinks—served quite well for those who would pay for the two-hour show. Stand-up comedy on television helped to fuel the coming of live club comedy. A & E's *An Evening at the Improv* became the enduring model for such shows. I would—and still do—go to a comedy club and marvel that individuals could stand on a bare stage in front of a microphone for up to forty-five or fifty minutes, doing nothing but talking—talking to a house full of people who had paid upwards of $15 apiece, not including their refreshments, to listen to that talking. What they were paying for, of course, was the fun of laughter, which is what the person on the bare stage seemed to know how to provoke, somewhat on cue; or so it seemed. Moreover, if the evening's laughter had been particularly good, those same people would pay their $15 to $20 the following week to come back and go through the process again, with even different people doing the talking.

For the preacher, also a professional talker, something was going on here that I wanted to know a lot more about. I wanted people to crowd into my church to hear me talk, just talk; and after twenty-five or thirty minutes had gone by I wanted them to be disappointed that I was stopping; and I also wanted them to come back next week and pay, say, $20 for the privilege of hearing me talk again. It was a fantasy, to be sure, and I knew that I was expected to talk about different things and in different ways than did those comedy club performers. After all, mine was serious and theirs wasn't. Mine was about the real issues of living, and theirs wasn't. Mine was about spiritual matters, and theirs wasn't. Ironically, though, the more I thought about what many of the really good comedians actually were saying, the more I realized that we were not as far apart as I might have wished. They, too, often talked about serious things, about real issues of living and getting along, and about things that occasionally even bordered, if not on the spiritual, at least on a search for the spirit in human affairs.

More than thirty years ago, a reporter wrote a study for the *Los Angeles Times* in which he quoted a review of a performance by, of all people, Lenny Bruce, the comedian who, despite his notoriety, broke all sorts of barriers with his incisive comedy routines. The reviewer wrote: "He was a sweet, peaceful and beautiful man. We used to go sailing on the bay and Lenny would sit and write poetry about love and beauty—and about his own frustrations. I don't think he was a comedian, really, I think he was a preacher." Good comedians often get a lot of preaching done. In the midst of the laughter, something comes through a comedian's work, something that one really does believe, something that one passionately wants to have heard. And good comics are master communicators, subtle masters, in many cases, of getting themselves heard. I am in no way suggesting that preachers should, or even can, imitate stand-up comedians. Yet comedians and preachers have enough in common, both vocationally and by natural inclination, that what comedians have to learn the hard way, just to make it in the profession, preachers would do well to pay heed to. There are four principles of public speaking, public address—preaching—which the preacher can seriously learn from the stand-up comedian.

The Call to Spontaneity

First, if what the preacher says is to be effective in reaching an audience, it must sound unmistakably *spontaneous*. It is the rule of the stand-up comic. It is also, perhaps not surprisingly, the number one rule of every college course in Speech 101. It is also the unbreakable and unalterable rule of Comedy Speaking 101. Almost universally—and I want to take the "almost" away—people do not like to be read to. If they put up with it over any length of time, it is out of habit or some devotion to tradition or because something else in the program holds them in place. People are not comfortable being read to. There is something very tedious about being read to. Attention is hard to focus and maintain, not only for those listening to material being read, but even for the reader. It is too rote, too canned, too boring. Granted, all of us can put up with it for short periods of time, particularly when the material is intensely interesting to us. But not for a sustained period of time. As someone who has taught public speaking in college for more than two decades, I can tell you that there is only one way, really, to get a failing grade, and that is to read your speech to the class. Public speaking, aside from formal kinds of statements or pronouncements, is, by definition, extemporaneous speaking, spontaneous speaking. And if this is true for normal public speaking, it is particularly the case for comic speech. As Gene Perret, the comedy guru, has put it:

> When comedy is performed well, it appears spontaneous—as if it just popped into that comic's head. It looks easy. Good material is designed to give the impression that this performer walked onstage and thought these jokes up as he or she went along. We writers noticed that when we did our jobs

exceptionally well, no one knew we were even there. The better our jokes were, the more they seemed like extemporaneous bons mots.[1]

Saying this is necessary since so many sermons over the last few decades in mainline Protestant churches are, and continue to be, read sermons: prepared manuscripts that are dutifully and painstakingly read by the preacher to the assembled faithful. The fact is, though, that, communicatively, that just doesn't work. At least it does not work if the congregants, those who hear the sermon, can tell that they are being read to. *And therein lies the secret to the process.* The problem is not—not—that sermon manuscripts are written, taken into the pulpit, and read at the appropriate time. The problem is that people figure out, usually easily so, that the manuscripts are being read to them. If one looks again at Perret's statement above, he actually says that the spontaneous speech is never spontaneous at all; it only *sounds* spontaneous. And that is what I said a bit earlier is the requirement of the effective sermon: that it *sound* like spontaneous speech. Just as public speech that does not sound spontaneous is not effective, it is also true that spontaneous speech that is *not* meticulously and rigorously prepared is seldom effective public speech either. That is usually public speech that gets lost, that rambles, that ends up meaning nothing at all.

Perret tells about being present over the course of a number of performances by Sammy Davis, Jr., in Las Vegas. At one performance, he overheard two patrons, one saying to the other: "Boy, that Sammy Davis is amazing. I never knew he could ad-lib like that." What Perret said he realized was that in every single Sammy Davis show, the ad-libbing came at exactly the same points, with exactly the same words and even the very same inflections and turns of facial expression; and they had the same effect as ad-libs every time. Perret says it sounded so wonderfully ad-libbed, so spontaneous, because it was thoroughly, meticulously prepared.

As far as the preacher is concerned, the question for the comedy sermon as for any kind of sermon is not whether one should use a manuscript, a set of notes, or nothing at all when one works in the pulpit. No matter what mode one chooses, the requirement is the same if one is to be as effective as possible as a public speaker: One must *sound* utterly and completely spontaneous. Every word must *sound* ad-libbed, as though it is being thought as well as spoken by the preacher for the very first time. And if this applies to the normal sermon, as it does, it applies to the comedic sermon all the more, since a part of the comic spirit itself is that it is an unpredictable, spontaneous spirit. It is a first lesson that every good comedian must and does learn.

This does not mean that one should never use a manuscript in the pulpit. What it does mean, though, is that one must become so good at using a manuscript that, from the congregant's point of view, it disappears. One must know the manuscript so well, and be so adept at reading it, that one can read it, whether line for line or word for word, and still give the full illusion that one is *not* reading it. No less preparation is required, though, of one who prepares and uses only a set of notes, however full or sketchy they are. Just like a full manuscript, the notes must reflect careful thought and organization, as well as a deliberate attention to language; when this is done, one can take the notes into the pulpit with a strong sense that one will speak spontaneously, that one *must* speak spontaneously.

Some preaching students, and I expect some preachers too, believe that one can combine these two approaches effectively. That is, they can *read* parts of their sermons, particularly the hard parts, and then break away from reading their manuscript to extemporize the easy parts, usually the stories they want to tell. Read a few paragraphs, stop, tell a story extemporaneously, stop, go back to reading, stop, tell a story extemporaneously again, stop, go back to reading, and so forth. As this is usually done, with the congregation painfully aware of the movement from one mode to the other, few things are more damaging to the effectiveness of the sermon. The congregation is virtually given permission to go away during the read sections, returning, as it were, during the extempore sections, going away again when the reading starts, and returning when the interesting, extempore process returns. It is a rule of audience response to public speaking. Strangely enough, in such a sermon, it is not the procedure itself that is at fault. As a preaching method, in fact, it has much to commend it. For it to work, however, those hearing the sermon must *not* be able to tell when the preacher is reading and when he/she is not. The read parts of the sermon must sound as extemporaneous as the told parts of the sermon are. The sermon, that is, must be seamless, and all of it must sound extemporaneous.

Preaching without Notes?

Some believe, and I am one of them, that the most effective kind of preaching is that done without manuscript or notes. This, of course, requires a considerable amount of work, though it is certainly possible to do it week in and week out in the pastoral ministry. It also requires that after one's outline (even the outline of a manuscript) is completed, one must take a couple of hours to commit the sermon outline to memory. This is not as difficult, though, as it sounds, since most of us have far more capacities than we ever give ourselves credit for, let alone tap into; usually what this requires of the preacher is a measure of confidence in oneself and one's ability to memorize, something that only comes when one takes the chance of trying it a few times. But—and this is the point—preaching without notes, while it does guarantee spontaneity, does not guarantee good preaching. Not by any means. Good preaching is still a product of spontaneity plus thorough and careful preparation, and not just spontaneity in and of itself.

I do know some preachers who prepare sermon manuscripts and then commit those manuscripts, word for word, to memory, even though they tend to be special occasion preachers and not every Sunday preachers. The requirement, even with this seemingly overdone procedure, is still the same, however: The preacher must be a skilled enough actor or actress to be able to deliver the sermon from memory as though it is being thought and spoken for the very first time, with utter spontaneity, despite every word being known in advance. As such, it becomes the fundamental acting skill of the stage or screen, applied, as it certainly can be, to the pulpit. However the preacher chooses to do it, the illusion of spontaneity must be maintained if one is to move audiences, congregants.

Related to this is the second principle that the preacher can learn from, or at least have reinforced by, the successful stand-up comic, and it is not one that "goes without saying." It is the tried-and-true principle that *practice makes perfect*. It is not that one actually practices one's sermon before one preaches it, though that is often a very good thing to do; but this practice is not so much before a mirror as it is the practice of speaking in a spontaneous fashion. The point is this: The more one practices the art of spontaneous speech, the better one gets at it, and this is true whether one speaks with notes, without notes, or with a manuscript. In fact, the instruction that is usually given to aspiring stand-up comedians is that the more they rehearse their act, the more spontaneous the act becomes; hence the more effective the act is, as far as the audience is concerned. This is invariably emphasized, since many would-be comics believe that "since they are naturally funny," they don't really need to rehearse very much what they plan to do. The principle is that one rehearses carefully, even meticulously, in order that the act—the sermon—can sound completely unrehearsed. It is the Sammy Davis, Jr., principle.

This, though, is more than just a matter of memorizing one's lines and being able to say them as well as ad-libbed lines. It is the difference between the amateur and the professional in virtually any human undertaking. That is, the amateur at whatever the activity is has to concentrate very hard on the doing of the activity itself—whether it is playing the piano and concentrating intensely on the notes written on the page, or playing baseball or golf and having to concentrate intensely and even deliberately on how one is holding and swinging the bat or the club. The professional, on the other hand, has practiced and practiced and practiced the fundamentals so long and so often that they become second nature. It is not that the fundamentals are less important to the professional than to the amateur; in fact, it is just the opposite. It is that the professional has worked so long and hard and knows the fundamentals so well that he or she can veer from them at will in order to do unplanned things. Someone can ask the professional piano player to change the key of a song being played, and without missing a beat, the arpeggio is made and the key changes—spontaneously. The amateur, however, probably cannot make such a change, since the notes on the page do not move that way.

The third principle of effective stand-up comedy from which the preacher may learn is that the comedian must ever and always be fully himself or herself when performing. It is the principle of *naturalness*. The comedian, the preacher, must appear to be fully and wholly natural in front of people. This is related, of course, to the seminal idea of spontaneity as a basis for public speaking. Granted, many comics are anything but themselves when they go on stage; they have an act, and when the houselights go down, shall we say, they kick into their act. That is not the stand-up comedian's way, nor is it what we are talking about for the preacher. Nor is what we are saying here related to the idea of following one's comic "persona," which we developed in an earlier chapter; that had to do with *what* one talks about, one's unique way of looking at oneself and other things. Here we are concerned with how one speaks to people; and the principle, well known to all good comedians, is to talk to a crowd of people as naturally as one would talk in a one-on-one situation with another person. The spontaneity of conversation—animated, alive, filled with intensity—is the model for the most effective public speaking possible.

Does that mean that in preaching one cannot raise one's voice, cannot turn up the heat and the volume, occasionally? Of course it does not. Intensity itself is not only animated but also greatly varied in pitch and volume. Does this criterion of naturalness mean that one cannot get caught up occasionally on rhetorical flights, flights of verbal repetition and cadence? It does not mean that at all; that kind of speech will always have its role in the sermon, as well as in other forms of public speaking. What it *does* mean, however, is that everything that is done by the preacher must have a *naturalness* about it, that what the preacher does in speaking must never seem contrived or forced, that it must, in a sense, always fit within the framework of the Preacher's personality and abilities as well as within the expectations of the congregants, the audience.

Being Responsive to Congregants

Finally, for the preacher in the pulpit, as for the comedian on the platform, it is fundamentally necessary to stay as responsive to one's listeners as possible. One cannot do this, of course, without a full sense of spontaneity, and without being, as we just said, completely oneself when one preaches. The fact is that one of the hardest things for a young comedian to learn is not *whether* to be responsive to an audience, but *how* to be. That is also the problem for the preacher. In fact, the matter is so important that Gene Perret's classic textbook on stand-up comedy has a chapter devoted to the problem of being in touch with the audience; it is titled, "Have a Conversation With Your Audience." It is followed by a chapter titled, "Take Charge of Your Audience." The point, and it is closely related to everything that we have said so far, is that one should *talk with* one's audience, one's congregation, even in the preaching of the sermon. Do not talk at them or above them or down to them, but *with them*. This is the principle, in fact, from which naturalness in preaching is developed. It is not an easy lesson for preachers to learn—the very idea that we are "preaching to" them seems to militate against such an attitude in the pulpit. Yet effectiveness, particularly in a comic sermon, requires it.

The idea of "talking with" one's congregation is an effort to point to another aspect of the speaker-audience interaction that the good comedian learns. It is that the preacher not only talks with the congregation, but *listens to it* at the same time. Again, beginners in preaching who get tied into their prepared manuscripts have no way to do this; so the manuscript preacher is pressed to become good enough with the manuscript and spontaneous enough in its use so that he or she can listen to the congregation at the same time, and can even move away from the manuscript when some response within the congregation requires it—something that is not at all unusual. This something is often an unexpected response to what one says—laughter, perhaps, where one did not anticipate laughter; or a clearly detectable mood of sadness or tenseness that the preacher did not expect, either. The preacher must not only be in a position to pick up on such audience responses—and they can change both quickly and noticeably in the course of a sermon—but also be in a position to take account of them, even if that means ad-libbing around some part of one's prepared sermon.

Good comedians in front of audiences know all of this, of course. Good comedians know that staying tuned to one's audience, listening, sensing, is essential to having people come back a second time for another show. Audiences want to be in touch with those who speak to them, whether in a purely entertainment setting or not. Audiences need some distance from the performer, to be sure, and theaters, clubs, and even churches are arranged to provide that distance. But if there is no reciprocal reaching across that distance, then the audience, the congregation, goes away feeling alienated, untouched. Which may account, at least in part, for why many people will go to a church once, but may not make it back for a second try.

The preacher, like the comedian, wants a reaction from the one who comes to participate in the sermon—for the comedian, the show. It is not that the preacher wants a specific reaction; in fact, the good preacher, like the good comedian, knows that one can neither program nor anticipate what the reaction may be to what one says or what goes on. But one wants to see *some* reaction, even if the reaction is subdued; it is a sign of life. As Gene Perret put it in instructing comedians:

> As a comedian, you usually want laughter. You certainly want applause. You might even be thrilled with some hooting, hollering, foot stomping, arm waving and barking like we see on "The Arsenio Hall Show." However, there will be times when you want silence. There will be occasions when you'll want a smile rather than a raucous laugh. Sometimes you'll be thrilled to see some of the audience choke up and perhaps a tear overflow from one's eyes. There are all sorts of subtle reactions that you may want from your listeners.[2]

To get such responses, however, the preacher must be in touch with the congregants—before and after the sermon, yes, but also *during* the sermon. That is where spontaneity and naturalness come together in the preaching of the comic sermon. That is where, and when, the sermon reaches across borders and boundaries with warmth, laughter, and genuine human emotion. That is what the comic sermon, preached well, is always supposed to do.

APPENDIX: Three Sermons

The following sermon by Fred B. Craddock is the one to which reference has been made throughout the preceding chapters. The sermon was published on both audiotape and in manuscript form in the Preaching Today sermon series, Tape No. 50, in 1987. It is reprinted here, with permission. The sermon is divided into the sequences that have been discussed at various points in chapters of this book.

When the Roll Is Called Down Here
Romans 16

INTRODUCTION

I hope you will not feel guilty if your heart was not all aflutter during the reading of the text. It's not very interesting. It's a list of names, a list of strange names. I always tell my students in preaching class, "When you're preaching from biblical texts, avoid the lists. They're deadly. Don't preach from the lists." It seems that Paul is calling the roll. That's a strange thing in itself. I have never worshiped in a church in which anyone got up and called the roll. It could be very dull. Well, it could...it could be interesting in a way.

SEQUENCE ONE

Calling the roll sometimes is not all that bad. Last December I was summoned to Superior Court, DeKalb County, Georgia, to serve on the jury. On Monday morning at nine o'clock, 240 of us formed the pool out of which the juries for civil and criminal cases would be chosen. The deputy clerk of the Superior Court stood and called the roll. Two hundred and forty names. She did not have them in alphabetical order. You had to listen. And while I was listening, I began to *listen*. There were two Bill Johnsons. One was black and one was white, and they were both Bill Johnson.

169

There was a man named Clark, a Mr. Clark, who answered when the clerk read "Mrs. Clark." He said, "Here."

And she looked up and said, "Mrs. Clark."

And he said, "Here."

And she said, "*Mrs.* Clark."

And he stood up and said, "Well, I thought the letter was for me, and I opened it."

And she said, "We summoned Mrs. Clark."

And he said, "Well, I'm here. Can't I do it? She doesn't have any interest in this sort of thing."

And the clerk said, "Mr. Clark, how do you know? She doesn't even know she's been summoned."

This roll call *was* pretty good. There was a man there whose name I wrote down phonetically because I couldn't spell it. His name was Zerfel Lashenstein. I remember it because they went over it five or six times, mispronouncing it. He insisted it be pronounced correctly and finally stood in a huff and said, "I see no reason why I should serve on a jury in a court that can't pronounce my name."

The woman next to me said, "Lie-shen-stein. I wonder if he's a Jew?"

I said, "Well, I don't know. Could be. Does it matter?"

And she said, "I am German. My name is Zeller."

And I said, "Well, it doesn't matter. That was forty years ago."

And she said, "He and I could be seated next to each other in a jury."

I said, "Well, you were probably just a child when all that happened years ago."

And she said, "I was ten years old. I visited Grandmother. She lived about four miles from Buchenwald. I smelled the odor."

SEQUENCE TWO (TEXT)

You know, a person could get interested in Paul's calling the roll. Even if it's no more than to say, "I wonder how Paul knew all those people since he had never been to the church?" I wonder if back then you could buy mailing lists? After all, he wants to raise money in Rome for his Spanish mission, and he is politically wise.

He says, "Tell this one hello and that one hello." Some scholars think this doesn't even belong in Romans. He's never been to Rome. But I'm interested in the roll call because it gives a kind of sociological profile of the membership of the church.

Now, I don't expect you to remember, but in the list there is a husband and wife, Aquila and Priscilla. There's a man and his mother, Rufus and his mother. There is a brother and sister, Nereus and his sister. There are brothers, Andronicus and Junias. There are sisters, Tryphaena and Tryphosa. There is an old man, Epaenetus. Isn't that an interesting profile of the church? There is a single woman, Mary. There's a single man, Herodian. Not a lot of nuclear family there at all, except as Christ has called them together. It's an interesting list, sort of. Not very.

SEQUENCE THREE

But for Paul it's not a list. Don't call it a list. He's packing his stuff. He's in the home of Gaius in Corinth, who is host to Paul and host to the church in Corinth. Paul is getting ready to go west to Italy and Spain. He's about to move to a new parish, one far away. He is now about fifty-nine years old, I would guess. He feels he has one more good ministry in him. Most churches don't want a person fifty-nine years old, but those churches had no choice, because Paul started his own. He wants to have one other ministry because he got a late start. He was probably about thirty-five when he started. He doesn't have much to pack: his coat and his books and a few things. And while he is throwing things away to trim down the load for packing and moving, he comes across some notes and some correspondence, and he sits down among the boxes and begins to remember. Don't call it a list.

SEQUENCE FOUR

You've done it yourself. When my wife and I finished our service at the student church when in seminary, our last Sunday there they gave us a gift. It was a quilt some of the women of the church had made, and they stitched into the top of the quilt the names of all the church members. And every time we move and we come across that quilt, we spread it out on the bed and we start remembering. We remember something about everyone—there's Chester, who voted against and persuaded others to vote against my raise. There's Mary and John, who put new tires on our car. There's Loy, very quiet, never said anything. There is his wife, Marie. There is this marvelous woman, Loyce, lived with that man who drank and became violent, and yet she was always faithful and pleasant. And he was dying of cancer when we went—my first funeral there, you remember. This is the way we go over the quilt. Don't call it a list.

SEQUENCE FIVE (TEXT)

Paul said, "Don't call it a list. Aquila and Priscilla, they risked their necks for me. Andronicus and Junias, we were in jail together. Phew! They're great Christians. There's Mary. Mary worked hard. She was there when everybody else quit. She's the one who always said, 'Now, Paul, you go on home; I'll put things up. I'll put the hymnals away, and I'll pick up all the papers and straighten the chairs. You go on home; you're tired.' 'Well, Mary, you're tired too.' 'Yes, Paul, but you've got to ride a donkey across Asia tomorrow. You go on. I'll pick up here.' Mary worked hard.

"Epaenetus, the first person converted under my preaching, and I didn't sleep a wink that night saying, 'Thank God. Finally somebody heard.' The first one to respond to the gospel. What a marvelous day that was! Tryphaena and Tryphosa, obviously twins. You hear it, don't you, in the names? Tryphaena and Tryphosa. They always sat on this side, and they both wore blue every Sunday. I never knew them apart, really. One of them had a mole on her cheek, but I didn't know if it was Tryphaena or Tryphosa. I never did get them straight. And Rufus. Tell Rufus hello, and tell his mother hello, because she's my mother, too."

Isn't that something? Some woman earned from this apostle the title "Mother." Can't you see her, this woman able to be mother to Paul? Probably stayed in their home. She was a rather large woman. Always had an apron, a lot of things stuffed in the pocket of the apron, hair pulled back in a bun. Fixed a good breakfast. Paul said, "I'm sorry. I can't stay. I have to be on my way."

"Sit down and eat your breakfast. I don't care if you are an apostle, you've got to eat."

Tell my mother hello—this is not a list.

SEQUENCE SIX

I remember when they brought the famous list to Atlanta. The workers set it up in the public place, block after block to form a long wall of names. Vietnam names. Some of us looked at it as if it were a list of names. Others went over closer. Some walked slowly down the column. There was a woman who went up and put her finger on a name, and she held a child up and put the child's hand on a name. There was a woman who kissed the wall at a name. There were flowers lying beneath the wall. Don't call it a list. It's not a list.

SEQUENCE SEVEN (TEXT)

In fact these names in Romans 16 are for Paul extremely special, because even though he says, "Say hello to," what he is really is saying is good-by. Oh, he's going to Rome, he says. But before he goes to Rome, he has to go to Jerusalem. He's going with the offering, and he's going into a nest of hostility. And so at the end of chapter 15, he says to these people, "Pray with me. Agonize with me, that I won't be killed in Jerusalem, that the saints will accept the money in Jerusalem, that I'll get to come back and be with you. Please pray." These are not just names.

SEQUENCE EIGHT (A)

Do you have a piece of paper? Well, use your worship bulletin. Would you write in the margin somewhere or at the bottom these words: "I thank my God for all my remembrance of you." And write a name. You choose the name. You remember the name. Write another name, and another name, and another name.

SEQUENCE NINE

Before I married and was serving a little mission in the Appalachians, I moved in my service down to a place on Watts Bar Lake, between Chattanooga and Knoxville—a little village. It was the custom in that church at Easter to have a baptismal service. My church immerses, and this baptismal service was held in Watts Bar Lake on Easter evening at sundown. Out on a sandbar, I, with the candidates for baptism, moved into the water, and then they moved across to the shore, where the little congregation was gathered singing around the fire and cooking supper. They had constructed little booths for changing clothes, with blankets hanging, and as the candidates moved from the water, they went in and changed clothes and went to the fire in the center. And finally, last of all I went over and changed clothes and went to the fire.

Once we were all around the fire, this is the ritual of that tradition: Glenn Hickey, always Glenn, introduced the new people, gave their names, where they lived, and their work. Then the rest of us formed a circle around them while they stayed warm at the fire. The ritual was each person in the circle gave her or his name and said this: "My name is ————, and if you ever need somebody to do washing and ironing." "My name is ———— and if you ever need somebody to chop wood." "My name is ———— if you ever need anybody to babysit." "My name is ———— if you ever need anybody to repair your house for you." "My name is ———— if you ever need anybody to sit with the sick." "My name is ———————— if you ever need a car to go to town." And around the circle. Then we ate, and then we had a square dance. And at a time they knew—I didn't know—Percy Miller, with thumbs in his bibbed overalls, would stand up and say, "It's time to go." Everybody left, and he lingered behind and with his big shoe kicked sand over the dying fire.

At my first experience of that, he saw me standing there still. He looked at me and said, "Craddock, folks don't ever get any closer than this." In that little community, they have a name for that. I've heard it in other communities, too. In that community, their name for that is *church*. They call that church.

SEQUENCE EIGHT (B)

Have you written any names? Do you have a name or two? Keep the list. *Keep* the list, because to you it's not a list. In fact, the next time you move, keep that. Even if you have to leave your car and your library and your furniture and your typewriter and everything else, take that with you. In fact, when your ministry is ended and you leave the earth, take it with you.

I know, I know, I know. When you get to the gate St. Peter's going to say, "Now, look, you went into the world with nothing, you gotta come out of it with nothing. Now what have you got?"

And you say, "Well, it's just some names."

"Well, let me see it."

"Well, now this is just some names of folk I worked with and folk who helped me."

"Well, let me see it."

"Well, this is just a group of people that if it weren't for them, I'd have never made it."

He says, "I want to see it." And he smiles and says, "I know all of them. In fact, on my way here to the gate I passed a group. They were painting a big, red sign to hang over the street, and it said, 'Welcome Home'."

The second sermon is by the Reverend Jane Voigts, a 1996 Master of Divinity graduate of the Claremont School of Theology; she is also a former professional comedienne. She is an ordained minister in the United Methodist Church and currently Associate Pastor of the Westwood United Methodist Church in Los Angeles, California. This sermon contains a bit of "show and tell," as she puts it; items are regularly pulled out of a bag and set up to create an arresting piece of sculpture, a representation of the Kingdom of God.

Fun with Rummage
Luke 18: 9–14

And now for today's sermon, "Fun With Rummage." Actually, I wanted to title it "Rummage Sale," since that more simply describes what I'm going to talk about today. But, I began to worry that if we put "Rummage Sale" out on the sign in front, where we always advertise the week's sermon title, throngs of people would show up today expecting a rummage sale and be thoroughly angry and confused that all we had to offer was this dumb ol' sermon. I know we wish more visitors would show up for Sunday morning worship, but if we did it this way, we'd undoubtedly have nothing short of a riot on our hands.

In any case, I did want to pay tribute to the great Christian festival that took place during this past week at St. James United Methodist Church: the annual Fall Rummage Sale. All year, you have been preparing for this sale, gathering tons of stuff from people all over the community, and you've been storing it in the back of the gym, on the stage, in closets, and all our unused classrooms, and in every nook and cranny of the church—and then, this week, you were diligently here night and day, pulling out all the stored stuff and setting it up in the gym, the lounge, the patio, the parking lot—it was wall-to-wall, ceiling-to-floor—stuff, stuff, glorious stuff!

As you can probably tell, I love rummage sales. I don't know about you, but I find them incredibly therapeutic. On those days when I'm feeling really down and sad and hating my life, it's time to go to a rummage sale or thrift store. At first, the adventure seems far from promising. I walk into the white elephant space and it smells musty and used, and I look around and everything is dingy and dirty and nothing looks at all worthwhile; but then, I begin rummaging. Digging through all the uninteresting and average stuff...and then...suddenly...I find it. My eyes widen and

I stop breathing for a second. I can't believe I found it, this incredible one-of-a-kind thing and it's in really good shape and it's scandalously cheap and *I* found it so now it's mine and—I just can't believe it! I start breathing again and look back on the table that once seemed filled with nothing anywhere near interesting, but now, as if fairy dust had been sprinkled all over the place, fascinating and valuable things are suddenly popping up everywhere. So I gather them in my arms—they seem to be calling out to me, "Jane, Jane, you must buy me, too! Imagine what I'll look like on your coffee table, in your library, at your next costume party...No one will be able to stop marveling at me—or you!!!" When I take my myriad treasures to the cashier and find that they cost me a total of about $5, I leave the rummage sale or thrift store so happy to have made such wonderful discoveries. Now I'm filled with lots of energy and hope, and I believe that at any moment I might be able to bring about world peace.

If you think about it, rummage can be divided into three distinct tiers, and to demonstrate, let me share with you some choice items harvested from this week's sale. The first and foremost tier is the one that contains good furniture, such as nice sofas, desks, lounge chairs, and so forth, good clothes, furs, collectibles. I myself don't buy much of this level of stuff, so I'll share with you the nice bookshelf that our senior pastor purchased. These top-of-the-line items claim the highest price tags and are usually the first to be purchased. Pastor John nabbed this beauty the moment it hit the floor. The hope of finding good stuff like this is what brings droves of people to your sale. I call this tier of rummage "the highly functional."

The second tier of rummage is the stuff that does not necessarily have much extrinsic value—it is not worth much money—but it has much intrinsic value. This is the the wierd stuff, such as odd toys and games from childhood and faddish things that once were very popular but now you can't believe anyone ever made it or wanted it. This is the rummage I LOVE to find. Like this wall clock that looks just like a piece of odd-looking wood until you look closer and realize...it's in the shape of the state of Iowa! Or this record album of Wink Martindale reciting poetry—perfect for that romantic date at home. Or this cookbook that contains nothing but recipes for toast! Or this giant homemade calendar for 1971 that is decorated with giant 3-D vegetables made out of felt and glitter. Who would think to make such a thing? Who would think to BUY such a thing? I call this tier of rummage "Not Really Valuable But Highly Interesting." VERY interesting.

The third and lowest tier of rummage is nothing but junk. It's the stuff that won't sell in a million years. Like this dirty, hand-made crocheted pillow—who knows who's slept—even drooled—on this thing? It was 25 cents. And here's a ratty old handbag. Also 25 cents. And what about this—a rusty, star-shaped gelatin mold—I think it's already seen its last "surprise luncheon." Five cents. And, last, and probably least, this pan handle. It was free. You set these things out thinking SOMEBODY, for SOME reason, might want it. Who knows—maybe some clever soul might want this pan handle so they can take it home and paint on it, "Souvenir of Oklahoma!" The reality is, of course, that no one buys the junk, so at the end of the sale, you end up boxing it up and throwing it out.

In his time, Jesus compared the Kingdom of God to such things as a mustard seed, a pearl and a party. But if Jesus were living today, I wonder if he would not also say, "The Kingdom of God is like a giant rummage sale!"? After all, do we not often feel like human rummage, worn out and used up by the world and stamped with a second-hand price tag that is much lower than our original worth—and is it not because of these painful, dis-carded feelings that we most fervently seek relationship with God? Perhaps, had a bunch of shoppers actually wandered into the sanc-tuary this morning expecting a rummage sale, that's exactly what they'd find.

And, like any rummage sale, I would suggest that the rum-mage in the Kingdom of God may be divided into three tiers. There's the highly functional set—filled with church leaders and successful people. We admire and emulate the members of this tier, and they are good for church growth because they naturally attract others and inspire them to join up. Every church hopes it has a sizable number of highly functional folks in the congregation.

Next there is the "Not Really Valuable But Highly Interest-ing" tier—the people who are capable and interesting, yes, but who are not too active in the Kingdom, because they currently don't have the time, or they haven't found the right niche for them-selves, or they are too young to take on any responsibility, or they are too old and tired to lead as they did in the past. Persons in this tier are often highly lovable and we get great enjoyment from the time and energy spent connecting with and helping them. A lot of the ministry of the church is done for folks of this category.

And then there is the—well, one might as well say it—the junk. This is the tier, the group that is highly needy and doesn't give back much in return. These people require a lot of our time, and the effort we make on their behalf is usually not much fun. They seem hopeless and not a little bit out of touch, and if we are really honest with ourselves, life would be a whole lot easier if we could just put them in a box and get rid of them somehow.

Ah, yes, the Kingdom of God is like a giant rummage sale. And the good news that Jesus taught us is that GOD LOVES RUMMAGE! However, Jesus went on to say, God is not your ordinary thrift sale shopper. Most everyone else enters the sale and immediately begins salivating over the great furniture and high profile items being offered, while others like me are seeking out such spiritually transformative vehicles as "The Partridge Family Board Game." But God is like the shopper who makes a beeline to the rusty star mold and the ratty handbag, and she gathers them in her arms and becomes so excited and grateful to have found them that her eyes light up over all the other stuff, and she wants to buy it all—*even* the nice sofabeds and TV sets. Can you imagine being the rummage sale cashier, and this person comes up to you and gleefully exclaims, "I can't believe I found this dirty plastic cup. Do you know how long I've been looking for one?" We'd think whoever that was was pretty loco.

But that's the God Jesus knew. That's the God Jesus embodied. The God who loves all, but especially the dingy, useless junk. That's why Jesus, according to the gospels, spent most of his time befriending and hanging out with prostitutes, lepers, widows, aliens, the poor, and last, and perhaps least, the toll collectors.

Toll collectors were among the most despised people of Jesus' community. They did nothing but make everyone's life miserable and, oh, if only they could just be put in a box and discarded somewhere. Toll collectors were not tax collectors. Both extracted inordinate sums of money from the Israelite people to pay for the "privilege" of having the Roman empire control their land, but tax collectors were Roman bigwigs who oversaw the collection of large taxes such as the land tax and the census tax, whereas toll collectors were hapless locals who were responsible for bleeding the people on a much more petty level—charging them every time they used a Roman road or bridge. Except for Zaccheus, whose job approximated that of a wealthy tax collector, scripture really means to tell us that it was the toll collectors, a group much more lowly in social standing, that Jesus emphatically embraced.

Toll collectors were hated even more than the tax collectors, because they were considered traitors. They were shunned. They were labeled "unclean," partly because they dealt directly with Gentiles, but mostly because their work was so inherently dishonest. The only way a toll collector could make himself righteous in the eyes of his community and before God was to quit his job and pay back everybody to whom he had ever charged a toll, plus make considerable restitution to the temple. Of course, this was impossible, so the toll collector was faced with living life as junk rummage, about as worthless in the eyes of society as a broken, leftover pan handle.

And yet, according to Jesus, the toll collector was the hero of a parable. Luke tells us that the disciples were beginning to feel self-righteous and were holding the behavior of others in contempt. So Jesus told them a story about what happened to two men praying in the temple, in the Kingdom of God Rummage Sale. One was highly functional rummage, a Pharisee. Everyone wanted to be like a Pharisee. The Pharisee was a teacher of the law. So, while we may find the Pharisee's prayer from the parable ("God, I thank you that I am so great, and not like that 'nothing person' over there") terribly egocentric, that was the kind of prayer a Pharisee was expected to offer in order to educate those around him. Jesus' disciples probably would not have thought there was anything wrong with that prayer. What would have startled them, though, and perhaps even made them a little mad, was that Jesus moved their attention away from the esteemed rummage over to the east wall of the temple, the place where the unclean had to stand to say prayers. He pointed to the "junk" person who was beating his breast, hanging his head, and wanting nothing more than for God to become right with him. "Yes," Jesus said, "there is the man to whom God responds more than the other."

The parable ends there, and we don't know what happened next. But we can imagine that Jesus' disciples may have been quick to counter: "That isn't fair! That toll collector rips us off! You don't tell us that he then goes home and promises never to sin again. This doesn't make sense. How could God respond to someone so low and dirty?" Perhaps in the silence that followed, or more likely in the days that followed, the disciples were forced to realize that what Jesus was saying, in part, was that God loves junk rummage more than we know; that God stays on the lookout for junk rummage, that God really does find great value in junk rummage.

Although there is no direct counterpart to the toll collector in contemporary western society, there certainly are heaps of junk rummage which most of us ignore or disdain or seek to discard. Think, perhaps, of a homeless man, rather young, who has just seated himself in the back pew a half hour before worship is to start. We've seen him before, begging at the entrance ramp to the freeway with a sign that says, "Will work for food." We've never believed it and we try to avert our eyes from him and his sign. We've even seen him in the church parking lot after worship, asking for handouts from guilt-ridden parishioners. But here he is in church! He may even disrupt worship, while the rest of us are trying to listen to our pastor's intelligent sermon. "Isn't that just like those homeless people," we mutter to ourselves. "And besides, he's not really sorry for his sins; he'll be back on the street making a nuisance of himself the minute he leaves here."

How startling would it be for Jesus to walk into the sanctuary at that point and interrupt the service himself: "Pastor, stop your sermon for a moment. All of you, turn around and listen to this homeless man. He's got it right. There are some very important things you can learn from him." Jesus' words would undoubtedly make us very uncomfortable, even a little angry. "Yeah, right; what does this fellow have to teach us?" But if we look closely at this man, at his plight, at his fumbling efforts to make himself heard, if we really try to do that, we might somehow become aware of the depth of his desire to be touched by God. Or by someone. We might come to see this homeless man, and thousands like him, in a different light—as someone not so much to be changed as someone who can profoundly change us. We might come to see him as a blessed and scandalously valuable messenger, and member, of God's Kingdom. Think about that. Don't be too hasty here.

Perhaps that's the point of the parable after all; or at least one of its points. The Kingdom of God is like a giant rummage sale...and that's great. At this sale we find some highly functional rummage, and we are glad about that. In fact, some of us ARE it. At this Kingdom Rummage Sale we also find some delightfully odd and eccentric rummage; and, yes, some of us are IT, too. But the *really* Good News is that at this Kingdom Rummage Sale we also find lots and lots of seemingly useless rummage. And *that* may be the rummage that can actually lead us to salvation. Thanks be to God for that. Amen.

This third sermon is by the author of this book. It was originally preached as one of a series of sermons through the book of Revelation. Its subject is a profoundly serious and complex one, yet an effort is made to season it with the comic spirit without trivializing it in any way.

Sizing Up the Beasts

Revelation 12, 13

What a Story! This text from Revelation conjures up giant dragons and beasts from other worlds, metaphoric animals able to destroy whole sections of galaxies with the swish of a tail, beasts and dragons and behemoths and leviathans, reptilian-like creatures that go to war against each other, creatures with—what was it?—seven heads and ten horns, or ten heads and seven horns, creatures that rise up out of the sea or out of the land, beasts with heads like lions and feet like a bear's, beasts that breathe out fire.

It is difficult to feel anything but awe at the dynamic imagination that produced this writing with its heady mix of cosmic splendor and terror. Here is the unspeakable being spoken, the dark and awful reaches of death called up for the living, a nightmare verbalized in the daylight. Ironically, this is also comic writing of the highest order. Here is the *Star Wars* saga of the first and second centuries. Greek mythology christianized. Here are the space age comics, video games, dungeons and dragons. Here are the Superheroes and the Supermonsters. Here the world is not just black and white; it is technicolor black and white, filled with all of the horror, gore, and gallactica that Hollywood's best could possibly dream up.

But while the writing—scholars call it apocalyptic, as in *Apocalypse Now*—while it may have a distinct comic edge to it, which it does, it is also profoundly serious. It is an effort to talk about evil, and it is very difficult for us to know how to talk about evil in our world, very difficult for us—for humans past or present—to know how to even conceptualize evil. Oh, we can describe it sometimes; we can take pictures of it, but still, it is difficult for us to grasp it, to get hold of it, to experience it on its most monstrous scales, or even, at the other end of the scale, on its subtlest, smallest, and yet no less pervasive scales. So while the beasts are metaphorical, they are certainly not abstract. The beasts and dragons, those demonic, Satanic creatures, were the

Romans and the Roman Empire; they were Caesar and his armies. For Christians, the dark days of arrest, torture, and murder had arrived. Evil was rearing its monstrously ugly head and swishing its deadly tail through both earth and heaven.

Evil is as difficult to think about, to conceptualize, to understand, today as it was then. Most of our efforts to do so concentrate on evil at two levels, levels that were certainly in the mind of the writer of the apocalypse. The first is what we know as institutionalized evil. It is evil that becomes a part of the very fabric of a social or political order, or some part of that order. It is the evil that was Roman and that persecuated and murdered Christians. It is the evil of oppression, as when a minority in power holds masses of human beings in servitude. It is organized evil, the evil of military power run amok. It is the evil of the Nazis and the extermination camps, not only in the first century with its barbarian hoards, but in the twentieth century with its technological forms of genocide. It is the evil of the Japanese torture and massacre of 300,000 Chinese civilians who swept through the city of Nanking in 1937—a story finally documented in a new book by Iris Chang, called *The Rape of Nanking*. She calls it the forgotten holocaust of World War II. It is the evil described in last week's newspaper, whether in another story of a massacre of civilians in Rwanda or the murder of Roman Catholic Bishop Juan Conedera, head of the Guatemala City archdiocese's human rights office; just a few days before his head was crushed with a concrete block, he had issued a scathing report on human rights violations carried out by both sides in Guatemala's long civil war. The nameless, faceless, institutional beasts of evil. They still roam the earth today as they have in centuries past.

The second kind of evil that haunts us are the Big Beasts with faces. They are the Caesars and the Hitlers, those vicious individuals with vast power at their disposal, yes. And we wonder about the relationship between their power and their evil. But on a different scale, too, there are the mass killers, though whose only power is the deadly weaponry at their disposal. Often, even, without much weaponry. Just unthinkable evil in their hearts and the wherewithall to carry it out. When I was a young newspaper reporter, I remember when they began uncovering the bodies of young boys, really young kids, under the house of John Wayne Gacy in Chicago. By the time they stopped digging, they had uncovered more than thirty youngsters that he had murdered. Why?

The Hillside Strangler in Los Angeles killed young woman after young woman. Why? Jeffrey Dahmer lured young people to his apartment, torturing them, killing them, and finally dismembering them. Why? Teenagers now with guns, opening fire in school, killing three classmates in Paducah, Kentucky—Paducah, Kentucky?—another three or four in rural Arkansas? Why? What is going on?

What kinds of beasts are living among us—Big Beasts, terrifying beasts? Beasts with faces and names. We see their pictures. We know what they have done. We turn law enforcement on them. We hope a reactivated death penalty will finally put an end to such evil. So we execute the Hillside Strangler and John Wayne Gacy, and we feel relief when Jeffrey Dahmer is murdered in prison, and we try to figure out whether children who commit mass murder should be treated as adults or not.

After Jeffrey Dahmer was finally caught and put away, I remember tuning in on Oprah one afternoon for her interview with Dahmer's father. That would surely be a way to finally get some answers to the kind of mass killer that Dahmer was. Instead, it was an interview with a kindly, sincere man, one who reminded me of my own dad. He told Oprah with both grief and horror that he had no idea what went wrong with Jeffrey. He obviously did something very wrong someplace along the line, he said, but he did not know what or where or how. I believed him. He didn't know. And I came away from that sure that he probably did not cause the evil within his son. I came away wanting Oprah to set up an interview with the beast itself, or himself. "Tell me, beast, how did you get into this beastness"—or something like that. Oprah is not bad at getting answers, and maybe she could help. We need answers, but all of the talk shows hosts and all of the shrinks in the world seem unable to provide us with any.

Just a few weeks ago I was in a fast food restaurant and overheard a group of four young people—they appeared to be college age—talking very animatedly about the killing of the teacher and two students in the Jonesboro, Arkansas, schoolyard, the one carried out by the eleven-year-old and the thirteen-year-old. Their conversation centered on a theory that they all found very plausible: that the devil picked certain people to take up residence in, and those people, whether they liked it or not, became the evil people. Their new insight, in that jack-in-the-box conversation, was that the devil seemed to be making choices among younger and younger people. If you're picked by the devil, you cannot help it. You will kill as much as you are instructed to kill. There are voices in the heads of those who kill; there have to be voices, and the voices are those of the devil. Something in me wanted to go over and argue against the theory of those kids, to join their conversation and somehow correct such simple-minded, naive thinking. But I couldn't do that. I sat there realizing how much sense their devil theory actually made when you came right down to it.

I have a good friend back in the Midwest who specializes in training lay Christians to carry out ministry within prisons and jail settings. It's a complicated business, and one has to learn how to do that. He was preparing a videotape series designed to provide that instruction, and he took me on as the director of that series of video programs. As a part of that process, he lined up interviews with three prisoners on death row—on death row—at the Tennessee State Penitentiary just outside of Nashville. We would be in the penitentiary for two full days. I have never been subjected to such procedures as we went through to get not just all of our camera equipment, but even ourselves into that prison's inner sanctum. Search upon search, clangy door upon clangy door. Finally we were in a room—a large cage, really. We got our lights set up, cameras positioned, everything ready, and Tom, my friend, disappeared. When he returned, he had Frank with him, a prisoner a few months from scheduled execution, who had been convicted of killing two police officers in the course of a botched armed robbery. I don't know what I was expecting. I do know that the butterflies I was feeling in my stomach were not caused by being afraid of anything; they were caused, instead, by a vague sense that I was finally going to be able to look—I was very conscious of this—into the face of evil. I was going to be up-close, and I was determined to look deeply into the eyes and the expressions of this killer in order to get some sense of what made him tick, of what made him what he was.

The interview began. Tom sat just outside of the lights. Frank sat about six feet away under the full glare of the lights. Frank was young, in his mid-thirties, not large but muscular and very good-looking, clean-shaven, with an easy smile, a sly smile, really, with deep-set, piercing eyes. I could walk around, so I moved up close since I knew that under those lights he could not see me. I knelt down. I peered. I studied his face. I heard him describe how he had shot those two cops; he told it all matter-of-factly; and he talked about being visited by a preacher in prison and how he had given his life to Christ, and now he was forgiven, and he was ready to die. I didn't trust the words. I don't know if my friend Tom did or not; he said later that he was ambivalent about that. But I didn't. I wanted to know what was behind that handsome, but oddly upsetting face. I wanted to get inside that. Needless to say, I guess, I didn't. I came away skeptical about the words that had been said. I don't know why, exactly; maybe that says more about me than it does about that man on death row. We interviewed two others on death row, neither of whom made the deep impression on me that Frank did. Faces, I realized, often do not tell the story of what is behind them. Frank could have gone with us to Denny's for coffee afterward; but would we have wanted that? I wish I knew.

The following day, though, late in the afternoon, as our van was loaded and we were driving away, I looked back at that great medieval castle of a building in the yard of that penitentiary and I remember thinking to myself: I am glad I am not staying there. I am glad that I am not like those people in there, people like Frank. In a sense, I was thinking, and crying out within myself, that I am glad I am not a beast, with a capital B. I am not a Beast. That is not me. I can contemplate evil and search for its meaning on a variety of levels, but I am not evil. I am not one of the Beasts of our world. And that, I suspect, is you, too. You are not a beast, you who sit with me here today. We are not evil—are we?

Certainly we are not in any of the senses conjured up by the Great Beasts of Revelation. They may be all around us still, but, well, *we* are different. That is a fair statement. It is a true statement, and we need to say it and remember it and be honest about ourselves. But—let's slow down, too. Saying what we are not may be a bit too easy. It may get us off the hook just a little too quickly. Does this mean that there is no evil in us? That we are absolved? That we have nothing to worry about, as far as our own lives are concerned? Is there another way for us to think about evil, one that might let us acknowledge, and even work against the Big Beasts of institutional and individual evil—but one that lets us think about evil on a scale that is more appropriate to what and who we are—those of us in this sanctuary today? Let me try something out on you. Our problem with evil is not, shall we say, the Big Beast problem, but we might describe it as the Little Beast problem. Our problem with evil, let's say, is more like a mice problem.

Has anybody here ever had trouble with mice? Is everybody here being honest about that? I may have had fewer problems with mice over the years than most of you because I have more cats at home than most of you have, or had. But when I was growing up, we had mice problems. You don't want 'em in your house. Something about them makes us all squeamish. You usually don't see them, even when you have a lot of them, but you know they've been there, and you know where they've been, because of what they leave behind. Their little tracks, shall we say. They come out in the dark. That's when they like to do their exploring, their eating, their—whatever they do when you are not around. Mice like it under things, usually in the kitchen, though under sofas and chairs and beds can be fine, too. It can be dark and you come in and flip on a light and you can catch 'em. But they scatter so fast and hide so well that you can't go after them. You can set traps, of course, but my experience is that most mice are a lot smarter about traps than those who set the traps think they are. You can catch young ones usually, but those older ones, those with, well, more experience, can pick the cheese off a trap without so much as a whisker on the trigger.

The evil that finds its way into our lives is like the mice. We don't have to put up with a loud banging on the front door, and you go to the door, open it and there stands a behemoth growling down at you. Slam the door, throw all the dead bolts and chains, and keep the evil Behemoth out. No, that's not us. Instead, in our lives, we walk into the kitchen, open up a cabinet and say—uh oh, the mice have been here. There are the tracks. I thought everything was clean, but I must have missed some things. There are parts of our hearts and lives where one can open up a cupboard or look under the sofa and find a spot of real hatred. Most of the time it's out of sight, but if you look in the right place, it's there. The mice are there. The tracks can be found if you look for them. I am not a racist—you and I can probably say that: We are not racists—but if one should walk into our lives and throw on a light at just the right moment, there are some bad tracks, tiny tracks, of racism. The mice are still there. And even though our friends and fellow church folk may not think of us at all as racists, if they were to look under the stove in the kitchen, well, let's hope they don't, because the mice still are there, still leaving their tracks.

I was in a meeting not long ago, ten or fifteen were there, my Christian colleagues. Things were not going the way I wanted them to. I was outspoken, and the more I spoke the more barbed my speech became. I was not only angry, I grew downright unkind. I am not an unkind person, but I was unkind, and I hurt some feelings around that table, and I knew I was doing so at the time I was doing it. Sure, I was tired—I told myself later. And I was a bit out of control—I told myself later. My mice had gotten loose. I had turned them loose around that table. Unkindness is not just a little fault; it is evil. Love is *kind*, Paul wrote to the Corinthians; it was near the top of his list. Evil comes as a Little Beast in our lives. But it is a beast, nonetheless.

That's us. That's us. It is not the Big Beasts but the Little Beasts that work their way into our lives and make us miserable. Something we should have taken care of, but didn't. A lie we told that no one, we tell ourselves, will ever discover; and we tell it to get ourselves our of some jam we've gotten into. A deceitful act toward a loved one who did not deserve to have us pull such a thing. On and on the list can go. Mice. Little Beasts. But when mice take over a house, when the Little Beasts are allowed to run rampant with no one concerned about them—whew!—that house can go bad fast.

What we are called on to do, it seems to me, in the midst of all of the Big Beasts of the world in which we live—and we have responsibility as Christians for battling against those Big Beasts. But what we are also called on to do is to take stock of the houses in which we also live our lives. We are faced with constantly searching ourselves, under the furniture and in the cabinets to find all of those little tracks of evil that sneak in when we are not looking and that mess things up. We can sweep the tracks under a rug or back under the stove, but the mice will still be there, and eventually the mice will take us over. So the next time—and it is going to happen—when you find myself in the midst of some little but pernicious sin, some little bit of evil of some kind, remember the mice. And when you see a mouse—or, better, when you come across mouse tracks in your life—what you'd better do, and do quickly, is to pray that the spirit of God will come in like a cat and clear the mice away.

Notes

Preface

[1]Garrison Keillor, *We Are Still Married* (New York: Viking Press, 1989), 217.

[2]Conrad Hyers, ed., *Holy Laughter: Essays on Religion in the Comic Perspective* (New York: Seabury Press, 1969), 6.

[3]Suzanne Langer, *Feeling and Form: A Theory of Art* (New York: Charles Scribner's Sons, 1953), 331.

[4]Ibid., 331.

[5]Ibid., 331.

[6]Ibid., 344.

[7]See Conrad Hyers, *The Comic Vision and the Christian Faith: A Celebration of Life and Laughter* (New York: Pilgrim Press, 1981).

[8]Harvey Cox, *The Feast of Fools: A Theological Essay on Festivity and Fantasy* (Cambridge: Harvard University Press, 1969), 149.

[9]Fred B. Craddock, *As One Without Authority* (Nashville: Abingdon Press, 1971), 91.

[10]Hyers calls Kierkegaard the first "modern" Christian to seriously examine the comic vision of faith. He cites Kierkegaard: "The more thoroughly and substantially a human being exists, the more he will discover the comical. Even one who has merely conceived a great plan toward accomplishing something in the world, will discover it (the comic)....But the resolution of the religious individual is the highest of all resolves, infinitely higher than all plans to transform the world and to create systems and works of art: therefore must the religious man, most of all men, discover the comical (from *Concluding Unscientific Postscript*, Princeton: Princeton University Press, 1941, pp. 413, 414).

Chapter One: The Controversy over Comedy in Preaching

[1]There is no need to belabor a documentation of this, since it can only be inferred by surveying the homiletical literature during the first two-thirds of the twentieth century. To get the flavor of this, one may begin with Karl Barth's short essays on preaching from 1932–1933, now brought together in *Homiletics* (Louisville: Westminster John Knox Press, 1991), trans. by Geoffrey W. Bromiley and Donald E. Daniels, with foreword by David Buttrick.

[2]Elton Trueblood, *The Humor of Christ* (New York: Harper, 1964), 10.

[3]Amos Wilder, *Early Christian Rhetoric: The Language of the Gospel* (Cambridge: Harvard University Press, 1964).

[4]See Dan O. Via, Jr., *The Parables: Their Literary and Existential Dimension* (Philadelphia: Fortress Press, 1967); in particular the chapter titled "The Comic Parables." Other works by Via and others followed that took up the "comic" theme. Via depended almost exclusively on the work of Nathan Scott for his distinction between tragedy and comedy, particularly Scott's essay, "The Bias of Comedy and the Narrow Escape Into Faith" (*The Christian Scholar* 44, 1961). This essay was subsequently reprinted in Conrad Hyers' book, *Holy Laughter: Essays on Religion in the Comic Perspective* (New York: Seabury Press, 1969).

[5]Harvey Cox, *The Feast of Fools: A Theological Essay on Festivity and Fantasy* (Cambridge: Harvard University Press, 1969), 139.

[6]Frederick Buechner, *Telling the Truth: The Gospel as Tragedy, Comedy, and Fairy Tale* (New York: Harper & Row, 1977), 66.

[7]Douglas Adams, *The Prostitute in the Family Tree: Discovering Humor and Irony in the Bible* (Louisville: Westminster John Knox Press, 1997).

[8]Conrad Hyers, ed., *Holy Laughter: Essays on Religion in the Comic Perspective* (New York: Seabury Press, 1969), 15.

[9]Ibid., 15.

[10]Ibid., 23.

[11]Ibid.

[12]Ibid., 127.

[13]Ibid.

[14]Ibid., 128.

[15]*The Feast of Fools* (Cambridge: Harvard University Press, 1969, 144.

[16]Ibid., 155.

[17]Ibid., 157.

[18]See Niebuhr's essay in *Holy Laughter*, 138.

[19]Ibid., 128.

[20]David Buttrick, *Homiletic: Moves and Structures* (Philadelphia: Fortress Press, 1987), 146, 147.

[21]Douglas Adams, *Humor in the American Pulpit* (North Aurora, Ill.: Sharing Company), 73.

[22]See Richard Thulin, "Because of the Woman's Testimony," in *Homiletic: A Review of Publications in Religious Communication*, 21, 1 1 (Summer 1996).

[23]*Holy Laughter*, 243.

Chapter Two: The Resurgence of Comedy in Preaching

[1]See Hugh Dalziel Duncan, *Communication and Social Order* (New York: Oxford University Press, 1962). While Duncan scatters comments about comedy and comic theory throughout this and other books, his discussion takes up about 100 pages in Part 8 of this book, "The Social Function of Art in Society." Many of the ideas elaborated here are based on Duncan's insights.

[2]Ibid., 407.

[3]Ibid.

Chapter Three: The Nature of the Comic Sermon

[1]Henry H. Mitchell, "Preaching in the Third Millenium: A Theological Word Toward Survival," in Academy of Homiletics, Papers of the 32nd Annual Meeting, Oakland, California, 49.

[2]It is this dimension of comedy that creates such a strong tradition of "blue" or obscene comedy. The comedic is deeply intent on mining the deepest thoughts and feelings of the human animal, and often those deepest thoughts and feelings are well outside the bounds of the "accepted" societies in which we live. For a comic to pull to the surface, as it were, those deep-seated, antisocial concepts or patterns of thought and speech is to create the nervous, but often raucous, laughter of one who has been "found out."

[3]Johan Huizinga, *Homo Ludens: A Study of the Play-Element in Culture* (Boston: Beacon Press, 1950), 14.

[4]Ibid., 25, 26.

Chapter Four: The Comic Story

[1]James Cox, *Surprised by God* (Nashville: Broadman Press, 1979), 33.

Chapter Five: The Comic Premise: Finding and Creating Incongruities

[1] All of the newspaper stories that follow here were clipped and are reprinted, with permission, from the Riverside, California, *Press-Enterprise* between December 14 and 23, 1997.

Chapter Six: The Comic Metaphor: Discovering What is What

[1] Richard L. Eslinger, *Pitfalls in Preaching* (Grand Rapids: William B. Eerdmans, 1996), 9, 10.

Chapter Eight: The Comic Persona: Being Somebody in the Pulpit

[1] Gene Perret, *Successful Stand-Up Comedy* (Hollywood: Samuel French, 1993), 164.

Chapter Nine: The Constructing of a Comic Sermon

[1] Derrida's famous essay, "Structure, Sign and Play in the Discourse of the Human Sciences," has been reprinted in many places. One may find it, for example, as the concluding essay in *Contemporary Literary Criticism: Modernism Through Post-Structuralism*, ed. Robert Con Davis (New York: Longman Publishers, 1986).

[2] Richard L. Eslinger, *Pitfalls in Preaching* (Grand Rapids: William B. Eerdmans, 1996), 64.

[3] Ibid., 65.

[4] See the *Los Angeles Times* for December 17, 1997.

[5] No one in recent decades has written more about the process of play and its role in postmodern behavior than Jacques Derrida. From his first widely read essay to which reference was made a short time ago throughout his more extensive works, play is an idea to which he has returned again and again. By the 1990s, the notion of play has become quite sophisticated, particularly in the literature of postmodern ethics. One can see this, for example, in the excellent study by Zygmunt Bauman, *Postmodern Ethics* (Oxford: Blackwell Press, 1993). In a striking discussion of play near the end of the book, Bauman writes: "Play is *free*. It vanishes together with freedom. There is no such thing as obligatory play, play on command. One can be coerced to obey the rules of the game, but not to play....This is perhaps why play remains so strubbornly non-functional. Were it to serve a purpose, were I to play 'in order to' bring about or protect certain things I or the others like or want me to like, there would be little freedom left in my act of playing. The act is truly and fully free only when truly and fully gratuitous" (p. 170).

[6] Huizinga, 1.

Chapter Ten: The Art of Preaching a Comic Sermon

[1] Gene Perret, *Successful Stand-Up Comedy* (Hollywood: Samuel French, 1993), 52.

[2] Ibid., 172.